MR AND MRS BEETON

by

H. MONTGOMERY HYDE

AUTHOR OF
"MEXICAN EMPIRE" "PRINCESS LIEVEN"
"JUDGE JEFFREYS" ETC.

With a Foreword by

SIR MAYSON BEETON K.B.E.

GEORGE G. HARRAP & CO LTD
LONDON   SYDNEY   TORONTO   BOMBAY

First published 1951
by GEORGE G. HARRAP & CO. LTD
182 High Holborn, London, W.C.1

Dewey Decimal classification: **926.4**

*Composed in Bembo type and printed by Western Printing Services, Ltd,
Bristol. Made in Great Britain*

MR AND MRS BEETON

MRS ISABELLA BEETON

At the age of twenty-one.

From a contemporary photograph in the National Portrait Gallery

Fr.

TO

THE MEMORY OF

SAMUEL AND ISABELLA BEETON

Foreword

by

SIR MAYSON BEETON K.B.E.[1]

To four generations of housewives Mrs Beeton's classic *Book of Household Management* has been a practical guide and daily companion. She married in 1856 S. O. Beeton, an editor and publisher of exceptional ability. They were mutually helpful in their literary work, and to his inspiration her own book, distinguished by its intellectual and interesting qualities, owes its origin. The mother of four sons, she died aged twenty-eight, leaving the memory of a good, lovely and gifted woman.

National Portrait Gallery

THE general knowledge of my parents' lives does not go much beyond this brief appreciation from the pen of Mrs Margaret Mackail, which appears on the postcard reproductions of the portrait of my mother at the National Portrait Gallery.[2] The original I was privileged to present to the Trustees in 1932, and, judging from the Press comments, it captured the public imagination perhaps more than any other of the new portraits acquired and exhibited there in the same year. I understand that the sales of this postcard show that its popularity continues undiminished.

[1] This Foreword by Samuel and Isabella Beeton's youngest son was written some years before his death in 1947. As it was originally intended to preface the present volume, the publication of which has been delayed, it has been thought fit to print the Foreword as it stands. Further particulars about Sir Mayson Beeton will be found in the Appendix.

[2] Since these words were written Mrs Beeton's great-niece, Miss Nancy Spain, has published her biography *Mrs Beeton and her Husband* (1948), to which the present author is indebted for a number of fresh details.

A curious sequence of events led up to the presentation of this portrait. First, an article appeared in the *Manchester Guardian* (June 19, 1931) in which the writer, though anxious to do justice to my mother and her work, wrongly identified her with a certain Miss Eliza Acton, the authoress of another cookery-book which achieved considerable popularity about the middle of last century. I wrote a letter to the editor pointing out this error, which he duly published. A little later I was able to supply a contributor to *The Times*, Miss Florence White, the well-known expert on the history and bibliography of English cookery, with some fresh facts which formed the basis of an article entitled "The Real Mrs Beeton" which appeared in that newspaper (February 3, 1932). Among the readers of this article was the Director of the National Portrait Gallery, who had informed me that the Trustees, if they were given the opportunity, would like to have a portrait of Mrs Beeton for the national collection. In July 1932 the portrait which is reproduced in this volume, a modest coloured photo of the sixties, was formally accepted by the Trustees, who made an exception to their usual rule against accepting photographs for exhibition on the walls. Its public exhibition, which followed soon after, was very generally noticed in the Press; and a large number of articles on my mother's life and work made their appearance. Mrs Margaret Mackail, wife of Professor Mackail, O.M., and daughter of the late Sir Edward Burne-Jones, kindly wrote the 'miniature biography' for the picture postcard quoted above.

For a long time previous to the public exhibition of my mother's portrait and the appearance of the explanatory postcard her figure had become almost legendary, although her name had long been a household word throughout the Empire. The question was often asked whether such a person as Mrs Beeton really lived, or whether the name was simply a convenient *nom de plume* employed by an enterprising publisher. Where it was assumed that such a person existed, it was natural that some curiosity should be felt about her life with Mr Beeton and the circumstances in which she wrote her famous book. I understand that the late Mr Lytton Strachey, for instance, was anxious to write a biography, and that he searched in vain for sufficient particulars of her career on which to base it.

Now that my parents' identity and existence have been established, I have been repeatedly urged to supplement the few published facts with such details of their lives as are available and not generally known.

My mother died at my birth. She was happily spared the pain of witnessing the suffering and misfortunes which befell my father during the few remaining years of his life. He died the victim of chronic phthisis in 1877. Their married life, though short, was a happy one, except for the loss of the first two children born to them.

"But four times seven years were all she passed in this world," wrote my father, in the touching words of the epilogue hastily added to the last work on which they were engaged together,

and since the day she became wedded wife her greatest, chiefest aims were to provide for the comfort and pleasure of those she loved and had around her, and to employ her best faculties for the use of her sisters, Englishwomen generally. . . .

Her Works speak for themselves; and, although taken from

this world in the very height of health and strength, and in the early days of womanhood, she felt that satisfaction— so great to all who strive with good intent and warm will— of knowing herself regarded with respect and gratitude.

Acknowledgments

THE author desires to express his thanks to the following for assistance willingly rendered in the preparation of this book: the daughters of the late Sir Mayson Beeton, Mrs Marjorie Kilby, Mrs Isabel Farebrother, and Mrs Audrey Levick, and his grandson, Mr Rodney Levick, for permission to make use of their family papers and collection of Beeton publications; the foregoing, as well as the Directors of the National Gallery and the National Portrait Gallery, for permission to reproduce pictures in their possession; and Messrs Ward, Lock, and Co., Ltd, for information which they have been kind enough to provide.

Contents

Chapter I. Three Victorian Families   *page* 15

II. The Boy Publisher   29

III. Courtship and Marriage   58

IV. Household Management   88

V. Good Fortune and Bad Fortune   112

VI. The Republican Movement   144

VII. Finis   158

Appendix: The Late Sir Mayson Beeton, K.B.E.   181

Index   185

Illustrations

Mrs Isabella Beeton *frontispiece*

Samuel Orchart Beeton *page* 26

Derby Day 27

The Cover of the First English Edition of *Uncle Tom's Cabin* 128

The Title-page of the First Edition of the Famous *Book of Household Management* 128

S. O. Beeton's Publishing Offices at 248 Strand 129

S. O. Beeton 144

The Cover of *Edward VII* 145

Chapter I

THREE VICTORIAN FAMILIES

TOWARDS the end of the eighteenth century, about the time of the French Revolution, a young man named Samuel Beeton left his native Suffolk and came up to seek his fortune in London. He bound himself apprentice to a master-tailor, and for a while after serving his time he was employed as a journeyman, living and working in the neighbourhood of Smithfield, which was then the centre of this trade. Later, however, he entered the victualling business. The Napoleonic Wars brought prosperity to Great Britain and the victuallers, who provisioned the ships and armies which carried on the long struggle against France. Eventually, about the year 1809, Samuel Beeton moved to Milk Street, Cheapside, where he acquired the Dolphin Tavern, and remained its respected proprietor and licensee for the next quarter of a century.

Samuel Beeton's father, John, born in 1734, was a master-bricklayer of Great Finborough, Suffolk. It is uncertain whether he migrated there from a neighbouring county or parish in consequence of the building of Finborough Hall; but the family probably had a long-standing connexion with Suffolk, for the name occurs in local records for several centuries previously. These records show that in 1770 John Beeton married Thomasin Hunt, of Stowmarket. Samuel, the younger of their two sons, was born in 1774. John Beeton died in 1810, and was buried in Great

Finborough Parish Churchyard. By this time Samuel had married Miss Lucy Lawson, of Hadleigh, and with his wife was directing the fortunes of The Dolphin at No. 39 Milk Street, Cheapside.

It is on record that Samuel Beeton took a prominent part both in city and trade affairs. He was elected to the Common Council of the City of London as one of the eight members for the Ward of Cripplegate Within. In 1821 the Friendly Society of Licensed Victuallers chose him as their Chairman for the year. At the conclusion of his year of office he was presented with a fine silver-gilt snuff-box "as a small token of the very high esteem in which he is held by the Gentlemen who have witnessed his urbanity of manners, exemplary conduct, strict integrity and unceasing perseverance" while presiding over that body. He also belonged to the Worshipful Company of Pattenmakers. At the same time his tavern became a rendezvous for the sporting fraternity of the city, a development which, as we shall see, was not without its effect on the fortunes of his family. James Smith, the original owner of *The Sportsman*, appears to have met him in this connexion, since he too was among those who spoke most highly of him.

Samuel Beeton took a great interest in all forms of sport, particularly the Turf, and this interest was shared by his family. It is generally believed to have been at the suggestion of his eldest son, Samuel Powell Beeton (1804–54), that the race for the Great Metropolitan Handicap at Epsom was founded in 1846. This $2\frac{1}{4}$-mile handicap, which is run at the Spring Meeting over what is perhaps the most picturesque race-track in this country, owed its inception to a characteristic social feature of the period. In those days betting on licensed premises was quite legal, and taverns such as The Dolphin regularly saw considerable sums of money change hands in this way. When the idea of this race was first suggested it was seen that a good entry could not be secured except with the attraction of sufficient 'added money.' Consequently subscription-lists were placed in all the taverns frequented by sporting folk in the City. In this way the City tavern-keepers helped to finance this celebrated race, which came to be known as "The Publican's Derby," a name which clung to it for many years. After 1853, however, other means had to be found of raising the 'added money,' since the Act for the Suppression of Betting Houses, passed in that year, made the keeping of these establishments an offence, and thus rendered the publicans' ingenious scheme impracticable.

The Dolphin stood near the corner of Milk Street and Cheapside, on the east side, bordering Honey Lane Market. Though now no longer in existence, it was for many years a popular resort for the wholesale drapers, many of whom had their shops and warehouses in Milk Street, as well as for the sporting folk.[1] Among those who took their lunch there daily was Joseph Chamberlain, father of the statesman. He conducted a boot-and-shoe-making establishment at No. 36, a few doors away, and he liked The Dolphin, as it was near his place of business. "Old Mr Joseph," as he was known, was "a delicate eater" and "not very strong in health." He used to have a special cut of beef, for which "he paid extra," and this diet was coupled with several glasses of port wine, which his doctors had recommended, in accordance with contemporary custom, as likely to benefit his constitution.[2]

---

[1] It was pulled down in 1878, when Cheapside was being widened.
[2] J. L. Garvin, *The Life of Joseph Chamberlain* (1932), vol. i, p. 39.

B

Samuel Beeton's eldest son, Samuel Powell Beeton, was the putative founder of "The Great Metropolitan." He also became in due course a Common Councilman and a member of the Pattenmakers' Guild. He carried on a business as a warehouseman in Watling Street near by for a time, helping his father as well in the management of The Dolphin. In 1830 he married Helen Orchart, daughter of Thomas Orchart, the prosperous owner of a bakery in the adjacent Wood Street. While the management of The Dolphin necessarily involved living on the premises, the Orcharts no longer lived "over the shop," but, like the Chamberlains, had moved across the river Thames to Camberwell, then a pleasant and airy suburb within easy reach of Cheapside. Their only son, born in 1831, received the names of Samuel Orchart. It was this child who was destined to become a successful publisher and editor, found a healthy periodical literature for the women and young folk of the country, and inspire his young wife to produce the best and the best-known book of household management and cookery in the English language.

Samuel Powell Beeton's wife died soon after the birth of their first-born, and some years later the widower married again, his second wife being Eliza Dowse, by whom he had another family. This explains the fact of the eldest son being brought up by his grandmother, Mrs Samuel Beeton. Meanwhile Samuel Beeton had handed over The Dolphin to his son, Samuel Powell, who in turn left it at his death in 1854 to his second wife, Eliza. Some years later Mrs Eliza Beeton married a man named Isaac Wyatt, who helped her in the management of the tavern. She was a kindly woman, and Samuel Orchart always remained on good terms with his stepmother and her children.

II

In the same street—at No. 24—there lived Benjamin Mayson, who was in the 'dry-goods' trade. Benjamin Mayson was not a Londoner, but a native of Cumberland, and had migrated in his youth from that county to the City. His father, the Rev. John Mayson, member of an old Cumberland family, was Rector of Great Orton and Curate of Thursby, while his mother, Isabella, belonged to the Trimble family, which had been settled at Dalston, in the same county, for several centuries.[1] Benjamin Mayson married Elizabeth Jerram, the daughter of William Jerram, who kept a posting establishment on the Portsmouth road, and died prematurely from a violent combination of pink eye and influenza, which his widow used to say that he caught from the horses. Mrs William Jerram's father was a stud-groom in the employ of the Duke of Richmond at Goodwood named Standish, who is said to have been responsible for the laying out of the famous race-course. On her husband's death Mrs Jerram ("Granny Jerram," as she was later called) came to London, where she opened a lodging-house. Among her lodgers was Benjamin Mayson, who, as sometimes happens in such circumstances, fell in love with and married his landlady's daughter. Both Benjamin Mayson and his wife could be counted among The Dolphin's regular customers. They had four children, of whom the eldest, Isabella, was to become famous as the

[1] Mrs Isabella Mayson's brother, Robert Trimble, married Margaret Tennant, sister of Sir Charles Tennant, of St Rollox, Glasgow. Sir Charles Tennant's eldest surviving son became the first Lord Glenconner, and two of his daughters married respectively Lord Ribblesdale and Mr H. H. Asquith, later Earl of Oxford and Asquith. See W. T. Trimble, *The Trimbles and Cowens of Dalston, Cumberland* (1935).

wife of S. O. Beeton and authoress of the *Book of House-hold Management.*

Benjamin Mayson died in 1841, at the comparatively early age of thirty-nine, leaving his widow of twenty-five with four children and but little money on which to keep them. A letter from her father-in-law, then in his eightieth year, written not long afterwards, shows that she was left far from well-off. Like her mother, she appears to have considered the project of opening a lodging-house.

> ORTON,
> *August 8th,* 1842

MY DEAR BESSY,

I am sorry the business you entered upon did not answer your expectations. Of the one you are going to begin I can form no opinion, as I am totally ignorant about it. You say you have seen a House which might answer your purpose. You do not mention the Rent, but I understand the first Quarter's Rent is to be paid in advance, and if the rent be high you will observe another Quarter's Rent will soon be due. Do you suppose you will be able to meet it at the time, as he requires a Qr. in advance? I am afraid he will be a sharp Landlord.

You say you want a little money. I think I can advance you 50£, if that will do. Since last Christmas I have had a great deal to do. As I was not able to do any Duty, I was obliged to engage a curate. I think I shall never be able to attend the Church again to do Duty.

If 50£ will be of any service to you, after you receive it, you must send me a Note, as I wish at my Decease to have something made up for your children, and the above 50£ was a part of it. I intended to make you an allowance yearly. But if I do too much there will be less afterwards. I assure you I am anxious to save something for my little grandchildren. I have my curate to pay Quarterly. I do not wish you to sell your house, and also not to lay out your money extravagantly. I hope to hear that you are doing well. Carefulness will do a great deal.

I am sorry to say I do not improve much, I cannot leave Home. I do not enjoy Company. I am best when alone. I was glad to hear that you and the little ones were well. Make my love to Isabella and Bessy. The other 2 do not know me. They are very well at Thursby. I have not seen them lately except Anne who was at our House yesterday. I have not had much of Anne's Company lately.[1] I want to know when Esther was born.[2] I have forgot. Write soon.

With Kind Respects I subscribe myself,

Yours sincerely,

JOHN MAYSON

Mrs Mayson,
  No. 24 Milk Street,
    London

The times were not too easy for the widowed Elizabeth Mayson, but financial security came two years later, when she married again. Her second husband was a well-to-do widower in Epsom named Henry Dorling, who had formerly lodged in Granny Jerram's boarding-house, and had been a close friend of her late husband.[3] She was a widow with four children, and he was a widower, also with four children, so that they were pretty evenly matched. Though it was far from being a runaway affair, they got wed over the anvil at Gretna Green, as their

[1] His granddaughter Anne, daughter of John Bartholme, of Thursby. He married Esther, daughter of the Rev John Mayson.
[2] Esther, youngest daughter of Benjamin and Elizabeth Mayson; born posthumously in 1841, died unmarried in 1931.
[3] Benjamin Mayson had stood godfather to Henry Dorling's eldest son by his first wife, who was consequently named Henry Mayson Dorling.

marriage certificate shows.[1] The bill for the refreshment of
which they partook at the local inn has also been preserved:

JOHN LINTON
GRETNA HALL INN
GRETNA GREEN
March 24, 1843

				s.	d.
Lunch and Ale	-	-	-	6	6
Whiskey, Gin, etc. -	-	-	-	2	4
Post Boy eating, etc.		-	-	1	0
Horse, Hay and Corn		-	-		9
				10	7

In due course the couple settled down to their new life in
Epsom, where Henry Dorling had a prosperous printing
business and had recently been appointed Clerk of the
Race-course. To remove any doubts as to the legality of the
Gretna ceremony they were subsequently remarried in the
less romantic atmosphere of Islington.

III

The name of Dorling, which is still well known in the
neighbourhood of Epsom, has figured prominently in the
history of the town and its famous race-course for over a
century. Henry Dorling's father, William, was the first of
the family to become known there. Like the Beetons, his
forbears came from Suffolk, but he himself started life as a
printer in a small way in Bexhill-on-Sea. A few years after

[1] Gretna Green was probably chosen on the spur of the moment, when they were
staying with her sister-in-law, Mrs Bartholme, in Cumberland. The latter's daughter
Anne signed the register as witness.

Waterloo, however, he decided to move to a locality which offered more profitable prospects. He chose Epsom, tempted largely by the possibility of being able to undertake the printing connected with the racing. The move was duly made, so the story goes, with printing-presses, children, and household goods all stowed away on the same wagon, across the rough roads of the Sussex Weald and the North Downs of Surrey.

William Dorling achieved his ambition. In 1831 he began to print the race-cards—"Dorling's Correct Card" —and the name of Dorling, printers, continues to appear on them. The printing of these cards naturally brought him into touch with the racing world, and he proceeded to invest some of his business profits in shares of the Epsom Grand Stand Association, which had been formed some years previously with the object of accommodating the public more comfortably during the race meetings. The Grand Stand, a large stone building with dining- and living-rooms under the seats and boxes, had been completed in 1830 at a cost of just under £14,000, and it accommodated nearly 5000 spectators. "This splendid building," as William Dorling wrote in a description of it, "may justly be considered the pride and boast of Epsom. The superior and long-wished-for accommodation this building will afford will doubtless be duly appreciated and liberally patronized by the Nobility and Gentry who frequent these great Races." The truth of this prophecy may be gauged by the fact that it was not found necessary to replace the Stand by another structure until nearly a century later.[1]

For a time all went well with the racing. The extension

[1] In 1926, when the new Grand Stand, Club Stand, and East Stand were erected at a cost of £250,000.

of the railway from Nine Elms to Epsom in 1838 brought hitherto unknown crowds to the course, while the presence of Queen Victoria and the Prince Consort to see the Derby in 1840 further increased the public attendance. But the great increase in numbers unfortunately included many undesirable characters. There were also suspicions that the racing itself was far from honest. These suspicions were confirmed in 1844, when the race for the Derby Stakes was won by a horse called Running Rein, who turned out to be a four-year-old named Maccabeus. In an endeavour to conceal his real identity, the impostor's owner was proved to have painted the animal's legs with hair-dye, which he had bought from a barber's shop in Regent Street. It was here that the newly elected Clerk of the Course entered the breach. At this time the leading member of the Jockey Club was Lord George Bentinck, who had unmasked the Running Rein scandal. After an exceptionally good attendance at the Summer Meeting in 1845 Lord George spoke to the Clerk of the Course. "We must try to do something to pull Epsom race-course together," he said. "Now if *you* would get complete control, Mr Dorling, I should feel that the future was better assured."

The Grand Stand Association, being concerned with providing accommodation for the public, took little interest in the actual racing, while the previous Clerks of the Course had not been concerned as to how the Association was managed. It remained for Henry Dorling to link the two bodies together as part of the general scheme of reform prompted by Bentinck. First of all he proposed, with the concurrence of the Jockey Club Stewards, that the runners should be saddled in front of the Grand Stand. In return for this attraction he suggested that the Association should subscribe £300 a year plate money to the Stewards for the Race Fund. In the event of the Association finding this sum too much, he offered to take a twenty-one-year lease of the Grand Stand himself at an annual rental of £1000, and give a personal guarantee to find the additional plate money required. The Association accepted this offer, and thus the way was open for Bentinck's reforms.

Lord George Bentinck, a younger son of the Duke of Portland, stands out as perhaps the greatest reformer in the history of the Turf. He began his innovations at Goodwood, and they were gradually adopted throughout the country. But at no race-course were they more welcome than at Epsom, where abuses were particularly rife. There they were made possible largely through the co-operation and assistance of Henry Dorling. At first Dorling was somewhat doubtful whether the proposed regulations could be enforced, but Lord George's characteristic determination soon satisfied him. "If the conditions are that the horses must be saddled in Epsom town," Lord George said to him, "never fear but I will enforce them." And he was as good as his word. The conditions in question, which still provide the basis of the racing code, are too numerous to describe in detail. Among others were the numbering of the horses on the race-card, the corresponding number being exhibited in the telegraph frame—the frame was Dorling's idea; the dressing of the jockeys in jackets, breeches, and boots of uniform design; the saddling of the mounts at a given place; and starting by the aid of flags.

The saddling of the horses in front of the Grand Stand proved a tremendously popular draw, since it enabled the spectators for the first time to view this proceeding in comfort and see the runners canter off to the starting-point.

Another innovation for which Henry Dorling was responsible was the laying out of a new course for the Derby
which was designed to enable those watching the race
from the Stand to follow the runners from the start to the
winning-post. This was the so-called Low-level Course,
which began on the low ground in full view of the Stand
and the winning-post and had a severe uphill pull for the
first half-mile.[1]

The principal reforms accomplished, Bentinck could
safely leave matters in Dorling's hands. He now turned
towards politics, and sold his racing stable. It was the
occasion of Surplice winning the Derby in 1848, a horse
that had once been his, that provoked the oft-quoted description of the big race by his closest associate in the House
of Commons. "You do not know what the Derby is," he
said to Disraeli, who had come to offer his sympathy.
"Yes, I do," answered the future Conservative Prime
Minister. "It is the Blue Riband of the Turf."

By the middle of the century Henry Dorling had become
a well-known character in Epsom and the head of a very
prosperous business concern. Charles Dickens, who saw
the race for the Derby in 1851, described his meeting with
the Clerk of the Course in an article which he contributed
specially to *Household Words*, the popular magazine which
he edited.

> The railway takes us in less than an hour to the capital of
> the racing world, close to the abode of the Great Man who
> is—need we add—the Clerk of the Epsom Course. It is
> necessarily one of the best houses in the place being—
> —honour to literature—a flourishing bookseller's shop. We

---

[1] It was used with variations until 1872, when it was superseded by the present
High-level Course. All three courses embodied Tattenham Corner as an essential
feature in their track.

SAMUEL ORCHART BEETON
At the age of twenty-two.
*From a drawing formerly in the possession
of Sir Mayson Beeton, K.B.E.*

"Derby Day"

Mrs Beeton's stepfather, Henry Dorling, who was Clerk of the Course at Epsom, provided the artist with facilities for the painting of this famous picture. He also suggested its title, which the artist adopted.

From the painting by W. P. Frith in the Tate Gallery

are presented to the Official. He kindly conducts us to the Downs. . . . We are preparing to ascend the Grand Stand when we hear the familiar sound of the printing machine. Are we deceived? O, no! The Grand Stand is like the Kingdom of China—self-supporting. It scorns foreign aid; even to the printing of the Racing Lists. This is the source of the innumerable cards with which hawkers persecute the sporting world on its way to the Derby, from the Elephant and Castle to the Grand Stand—Dorling's list, Dorling's correct list with the names of the horses and colours of the riders.

Incidentally, it was Henry Dorling who suggested to the artist William Frith the title of his celebrated picture of the Stand and Downs on the day of the year's greatest race. The artist had enlisted Dorling's help in getting hold of photographs from which he worked up the details of the scene with the crowds. But when it came to the question of what to call the picture the artist was frankly puzzled.

"I shall certainly not call the picture *The Humours of a Race Course*," he confessed to Dorling. "I don't like *The Derby*. Indeed, I don't know what to call it."

"Why not *Derby Day*?"

And so it was called. Shortly afterwards Frith wrote to the Clerk of the Course:

I am sure you will be glad to hear of the success of my picture (about the title of which I took your advice after all) which has exceeded my most sanguine expectations.[1]

It will be remembered that Henry Dorling and Elizabeth Mayson each had four children by their first marriages. Thus they began their new married life with eight children. Together they then proceeded to have thirteen more

[1] The picture was painted in 1858.

children. Now, the Dorling house in the Epsom High Street was unable to accommodate a family of twenty-one. As they came along, therefore, the youngsters were packed off to the Grand Stand, where they were looked after by Mrs Dorling's mother, "Granny Jerram." In this necessary task, as we shall see, the old lady was largely assisted by her eldest granddaughter, Isabella Mayson, the future Mrs Beeton. The children lived in the Grand Stand all the year round, except during the race meetings, when they had to be accommodated with various relatives and friends in Epsom.

"I am going to the Stand this afternoon," wrote Isabella on the eve of one of the meetings, "to assist in bringing down that living cargo of children into the town, where they will remain ten days."

Mrs Elizabeth Dorling died in 1871, and was the first person to be buried in the newly opened Epsom Cemetery. Her husband never recovered from the shock of her loss, and two years later he was laid to rest by her side. He continued to act as Clerk of the Course to within a few months of his death.

Such were the remarkable circumstances in which Isabella Mayson, perhaps the most remarkable of the 'Grand Stand' family, grew up. Epsom was, therefore, destined to play a large and significant part in her life. It was to mould her character and give her experience while still a mere girl of household management on an unusual scale.

Chapter II

THE BOY PUBLISHER

As already related, Samuel Beeton came up to London from Suffolk when a young man, and eventually established himself as a person of consequence and respectability in the City. When his son Samuel Powell Beeton married Helen Orchart, he appears to have handed over the management of the Dolphin Tavern in Milk Street to them. Samuel Powell Beeton had previously set up on his own account as a warehouseman in Watling Street, but henceforward he seems to have devoted himself to the Milk Street business.

Samuel Orchart Beeton was born on March 2, 1831, at 39 Milk Street. A year or two later his mother, after whom he received his second name, died, and his father married again. By his second wife, *née* Eliza Dowse, Samuel Powell Beeton had a family of seven children. Meanwhile the young Sam Beeton went to live with his grandmother at Hadleigh, where she had settled down after old Samuel Beeton's death in 1836, and was brought up by her. Little is known of his boyhood days, apart from the fact that he went to a private school at Brentwood, in Essex—Pilgrim's Hall Academy. He appears to have been a rapid and eager reader of all kinds of literature; when he was twelve years old his father presented him with an edition of the complete works of Shakespeare. He was also proficient in languages, and while at school won a prize for French in the shape of a biography of Napoleon written in that language.

On leaving school at fourteen young Sam Beeton was apprenticed to a paper merchant in the City. The seven years which a trade apprentice customarily served in those days seem to have passed agreeably enough for him. In fact, he contrived to have "quite a gay time," as he confessed in later years to a friend, pointing out, as he did so, "the window he used to climb out at night." In 1852, when he was twenty-one, he became a partner in the firm of Charles H. Clarke and Co., printers, publishers, and booksellers in Fleet Street, the necessary capital probably being provided by his father. Clarke himself was a binder, while another partner, named Salisbury, was responsible for the printing; and, until Beeton joined them,they seem to have been operating in quite a small way. Recently, however, they had begun to publish books under their own imprint, mostly reprints of uncopyrighted works. It was this side of the business, with its possibilities of development, which particularly attracted Samuel Beeton.

So far at least as new books went, the publishing world was very different in 1852, when S. O. Beeton entered Clarke's offices at 148 Fleet Street, from what it is to-day.[1] Novels were published in three volumes, and cost the reader who could afford them the sum of a guinea and a half each. The circulating libraries, led by the enterprising Mr Mudie, were only just beginning their vogue, which was subsequently so to stimulate the public demand for popular literature. The market was dominated by such distinguished authors as Dickens, Thackeray, Carlyle,

---

[1] The offices, which are still in existence, were on the north side of the street, beside the entry leading to Dr Johnson's house in Gough Square.

Macaulay, and Tennyson, who with occasional lapses remained faithful to certain well-established publishing houses. Messrs Longmans, Macmillan, Chapman and Hall, Smith, Elder, and Co., and John Murray were among the leaders in satisfying the public taste in books at this time. Bookselling was then a fastidious and gentlemanly occupation, and there existed between the booksellers and the publishers a pleasant relationship typified in the annual Trade Dinner. At the beginning of every season the publishers would invite the booksellers to a good dinner, with choice wines and cigars, at the end of which samples of each firm's new books would be circulated round the table. In this congenial atmosphere it is not surprising that large orders were sometimes placed. On one occasion over 10,000 copies of a new book by Samuel Smiles, of *Self-Help* fame, were sold in a few minutes over the nuts and wine. But although in those days there were no cheap Press, literary luncheons, wireless talks, and the like to boom the merits of a potential 'best-seller' and the production of new books was on a scale with which the reading public could keep pace, there was, on the other hand, a steadily increasing demand for low-priced literature.

As Lord Brougham put it, the schoolmaster was abroad. Since the passing of the Reform Bill in 1832 education was no longer the monopoly of aristocracy and wealth. A knowledge of the arts and sciences was rapidly coming within the reach of all who could afford the economical encyclopædias and similar aids to learning brought out by the new publisher of the period, whose prototypes were Robert Chambers, Charles Knight, and John Cassell. Others rapidly followed in their wake, taking advantage of

the current improvements in printing processes, and the
location of cheap and efficient transport for distribution
provided by the railways, to bring out inexpensive editions
of popular authors, particularly the classics. This latter
development had been inaugurated by a publisher named
David Bogue with the appearance of his "European
Library" of standard authors in 1845, and his example had
been quickly followed by such enterprising trade competitors as Henry George Bohn (who eventually took over
Bogue's "European Library"), George Routledge, and
Frederick Warne, the success of whose publications was
greatly promoted by the railway bookstalls of W. H.
Smith and Son. There was obviously a strong inducement
to printers and binders, on whom the publishing trade
depended, to profit from the demand for reprints and
augment their profits by launching out into publishing
themselves. Among them, as we have seen, was the firm
of Charles H. Clarke and Co., soon to be known as
Clarke, Beeton, and Co.

While Chambers's encyclopædias and Bohn's standard
libraries satisfied the grown-ups, little attention had hitherto been given to the literary needs and interests of the
young folk in this country. There was a notable absence of
suitable books and magazines for boys and girls, and in a
lesser degree for women. It is true that authors like
Dickens and Thackeray were engaged in editing magazines, and in view of their other commitments they did so
extraordinarily well. But these magazines, though they
were read by men and women alike, were primarily
designed for the adult male section of the community and
its interests. The women of the country, as well as its
young people, both boys and girls, could obtain few, if

any, journals devoted exclusively to their tastes. It was this gap in our periodical literature that S. O. Beeton was destined to fill.

But before we consider this achievement we must first notice a singular piece of good fortune which befell the youthful publisher at the very outset of his career in Fleet Street.

II

The initial success, in which young Samuel Beeton participated on his first appearance as a publisher, must be accounted as one of the outstanding *coups* in literary history. Not only did it produce a fortune for him when still in his early twenties, but as an international 'best-seller' it eclipsed all previous records, saving possibly the Bible. The work which created such a sensation, and which the firm of Clarke, Beeton, and Co. was the first to publish in England, was Mrs Harriet Beecher Stowe's celebrated romance of Negro slavery in America, *Uncle Tom's Cabin*. The story of the book and the part which Beeton played in introducing it to the attention of English readers deserve to be more widely known.

The fortunate authoress, who had experienced a bitter struggle with poverty and other hardships in her youth and early married life, was at this time approaching a middle age of far more material comforts than anything she had enjoyed hitherto. Mrs Stowe, *née* Harriet Elizabeth Beecher, was the daughter of a Calvinistic minister, typical of many in New England. The family atmosphere in which she was brought up was narrow and deeply religious, but at the same time intensely intellectual. In the course of her education she displayed remarkable talents, if

c

we can judge by the fact that at the age of twelve she wrote
an essay which was read out before a large body of
assembled scholars and visitors. The subject of this amazing feat was "Can the Immortality of the Soul be proved
by the Light of Nature?" She became an enthusiastic convert to revealed religion, and her faith maintained her
during many painful years of poverty, sickness, and prolific
child-bearing. Her husband was a professor in a theological
seminary in Cincinnati, and he wisely regarded his wife's
literary ability as a divine gift which must be cultivated
come what may. The golden opportunity was provided
by the activities of the slave-holding community which
resided in the Southern States of the Union.

At the time of the Declaration of Independence in 1776
slavery was considered to be a dying institution in the
revolted states, and for that reason no express measures
were taken to hasten its end. Some years later, however,
the invention of the collin-gin for separating seed from
fibre led to a great influx of slave labour into the southern
states. So long as there was a demand for cotton the
planters would be expected to support Negro slavery, and
they represented a powerful vested interest, in spite of the
growing agitation for abolition in the northern states. In
1850 the question came into prominence through the passing by Congress of the notorious Fugitive Slave Act. The
reason for this legislation was the desire to conciliate the
slave-holding states in return for the admission of the free
state of California to the Union. It gave to any slave-
holder the right to seek out and bring back into slavery any
coloured person whom he claimed as a slave, and it also
laid upon the inhabitants of the free states the duty of
assisting in these searches for fugitives. The enforcement

of the Act naturally led to many heart-rending scenes. One day Mrs Stowe received a letter from a relative describing some of them and containing this passage: "If I could use a pen as you can I would write something that would make this whole nation feel what an accursed thing slavery is." Mrs Stowe read the letter aloud to her household, and when she came to the words quoted she rose from her chair and, crushing the letter in her hand, exclaimed fervently, "I will write something. I will if I live."

This was the origin of *Uncle Tom's Cabin*, which was written in the winter of 1850 and spring of 1851, much of it apparently in haphazard fashion in the kitchen in the intervals between cooking and nursing her seventh child. Before it was complete it began to run serially in the *National Era*, an anti-slavery journal published in Washington, D.C. It did not at first attract much attention, and, in fact, it was not until it had appeared in book form that the demand for it became considerable. For the serial rights Mrs Stowe received the sum of 300 dollars, which must have been very gratifying, since she modestly disclaimed the honour of authorship. "The Lord Himself wrote it," she said, "and I was but the humblest of instruments in His hand." The book rights were secured by John P. Jewett, a Boston publisher, who agreed to give the author a royalty of 10 per cent. on all sales in America. The first edition of 5000 copies was accordingly issued on March 20, 1852. The edition was exhausted in a few days.

Among those into whose hands fell the first American edition was a young man in the publishing house of Putnam in New York. He was about to embark for England, and, having heard that the book was selling well, bought it the day his steamer sailed from Boston, presumably to read on the voyage. As soon as he reached England he sent his copy to David Bogue, the London publisher, suggesting that he might care to reprint it and send him a trifle for his pains. At that time the United States had not entered into copyright relations with England, so that English publishers were quite free to reproduce the works of American authors without any fear of being suited in an action for infringement of copyright. Bogue, however, was not anxious to undertake reprints of American works, and he refused it; but he mentioned at the same time, among others, a friend whom he thought might be interested. This friend was the brilliant engraver and pioneer of the illustrated Press, Henry Vizetelly, who was also a publisher himself in a small way. When he heard of the proposition Vizetelly thought it might suit "Readable Books," a series of volumes of popular literature, following the style of Bohn's and Routledge's successful publications, which he had been bringing out in association with Charles Clarke at the price of a shilling each, and which must be classed among the ancestors of to-day's Penguins. Vizetelly, so he himself tells us, at first hesitated whether to bring out a work at a shilling which had appeared in two stout volumes in America, but eventually, as he was preparing to go abroad, he handed the book to Clarke, stating his willingness to be responsible for one-third of the cost of a printing of 7000 copies to sell at 2s. 6d. each if Clarke's firm would undertake the publication.

A night was all that could be allowed for reading the book before the final decision was made. This course was rendered necessary by the possibility that the next incoming steamer from Boston would bring a passenger with another copy, which might be snapped up by a more enterprising publisher. One volume was, therefore, taken home by the firm's printer, Salisbury, while the other was entrusted to a young man named Frederick Greenwood, who was employed as a reader by another firm of publishers. Greenwood, who was later to become well known as a journalist, and particularly as editor of the *Pall Mall Gazette*, was only twenty-two years of age at this time. He afterwards remembered with pride how his opinion had been consulted.

On the following morning Salisbury sent in an enthusiastic report. "I sat up till four in the morning reading the book," he said,

and the interest I felt was expressed one moment by laughter, and then by tears. Thinking it might be weakness and not the power of the author that affected me, I resolved to try the effect upon my wife (a rather strong-minded woman). I accordingly woke her and read a few chapters to her. Finding that interest in the story kept her awake and that she too laughed and cried, I settled in my mind that it was a book which ought to be and might with safety be printed.

The youthful Greenwood was equally enthusiastic. So as to be able to concentrate on the book undisturbed he began his reading late that night. "At the end of an hour I was in a tremble lest the story should sink from the height it had risen to," he remarked later, "and from that point read on with a still growing confidence of admiration till I came to the night scene in which Cassy maddens Legree with fear. That chapter, after what preceded it, answered Messrs Clarke, Beeton, and Co.'s question conclusively in my mind." Next morning he handed his volume back to Clarke with a strong recommendation to "buy and print quickly."

Clarke agreed, and the book was immediately set up in type. However, it was felt that the text required some slight editing for English readers. Vizetelly, for instance, had suggested that Mrs Stowe's sub-title, "Life among the Lowly," should be changed to "Negro Life in the Slave States of America," and this was done. At the same time the proofs were given to Greenwood as they came off the press, and he was requested to supply explanatory chapter headings, which were lacking in the American edition. Clarke also asked the young publisher's reader to write a preface introducing the book to the English public, which Greenwood agreed to do, and which he subsequently signed with his initial, "G." "And a mighty fine piece it is, and if I remember aright," he recalled long afterwards, "partly in Lord Brougham's style and partly in Mr Carlyle's. However, I got two guineas for it, and the publishers got a good deal more."[1]

As agreed with Vizetelly, an impression of 7000 copies was printed, of which the first 2500 were bound in cloth, the size being crown octavo and the price half a crown. It appeared on sale about the end of April 1852; but, though advertised extensively, at first it made no stir. It was, in fact, not until a rival publisher, Richard Bentley,

---

[1] The following is an extract from this preface: "Good books, like good actions, best explain themselves; they most effectually storm both heart and head, their virtues drape them with greatest dignity, the less they are cumbered by eulogistic comment. But while, therefore, we may be content with merely introducing this good book to British readers, leaving them to discover what beauties and excellencies, what tenderness, and humour, and delicate pencillings have rendered the story so popular in the free states of America—the purpose of the book we ourselves have some property in, and in reprinting it must assert the claim. And not 'we' alone, as expressive merely of an editorial fraction, but the English nation and the British peoples, more than all nations and all peoples, dead or living, may assert the claim; for the purpose is to disabuse large communities of mankind of the belief that the Lord our God, when He gave dominion to man 'over the fish of the sea, and over the fowl of the air, and over the cattle,' bestowed this dominion only on prospective races of a certain colour, and included under the designation 'cattle' other prospective races of another colour."

announced his intention of bringing out a shilling edition that Clarke decided to forestall this inconvenient move by working off the remainder of the sheets in paper boards at the same price. The book immediately began to make its way, and by July was selling at the rate of a thousand a week. It was shortly before this that Beeton had joined the firm, and now large editions, doubtless financed by his capital, were quickly put out. In August the demand became overwhelming, and by the autumn the firm had produced 150,000 copies of the book, and, as the sales showed no signs of declining, were busily employing forty people and seventeen printing-presses in getting it out. Other publishing houses now took up the running, among them those of Bohn, Warne, Routledge, and Cassell, so that by the end of the year over half a million copies had been sold.

Two accidental factors, which are worth recording, contributed to swell the profits of the first English publishers of *Uncle Tom*. Most of the rivals in the field reprinted the book from Clarke's version, and not from the American edition. Here was a further stroke of luck for Beeton's firm. Although there was naturally no copyright in the text of the novel itself, on the other hand copyright did exist in Greenwood's preface, which the other English publishers had unwittingly incorporated in their reprints, no doubt under the impression that it appeared in the original version. Large supplies were already in the hands of the retail booksellers when the mistake was discovered, and consequently none could be sold until an 'arrangement' had been arrived at with Mr Clarke.

The rival publishers, who had reprinted Greenwood's chapter headings, fell into a similar if more awkward trap.

Those who had used the preface could easily cut out the
offending pages, but nothing of this nature could be done
with headings which were scattered throughout the book.
One of these publishers was Frederick Warne, who thereby
laid himself open to an action for infringement of copyright if he offered any of his copies for sale. The upshot
was that Clarke and Beeton, whose stock of sheets was
nearly exhausted, were able to buy up the whole of
Warne's edition at less than the cost of paper and print.
"Merely replacing one title-page by another," in Greenwood's words, "they filled their yawning warehouse with
an abundant supply of copies drawn away from a rival
market."

Shortly after the book appeared, and before it had begun
to make its way, Vizetelly went abroad, where he remained for several months. It was during his absence that
Beeton entered into partnership with Clarke and Salisbury.
On his return Vizetelly was somewhat surprised, to quote
his own words, that "*Uncle Tom's Cabin* had been, and
still was, the book which everybody was reading and
talking about." He appears to have had some difficulty in
obtaining from the firm what he considered to be his
rightful share of the profits, and at one stage he threatened
to file a bill in Chancery for an account of the sales.
Eventually he received £500 from the firm, which satisfied him, and his connexion with the venture thereupon
ceased. At the same time he surrendered, apparently in
part consideration for the £500, his interest in the "Readable Books" series, which now became the entire property
of Clarke, Beeton, and Co. So far as *Uncle Tom* went,
however, there was no obligation on Beeton's firm to give
Vizetelly such a generous sum, since he was really inter-

ested only in the first edition, which, as we have seen, had not gone particularly well. His share of the profits had been paid to his clerk on his behalf when he was abroad, a fact which he does not deny. He had no part in the large editions which were issued after Beeton joined the firm, and which he admitted were not financed by his capital.[1]

Now that the success of the English edition was assured, the partners agreed that Beeton should visit America and offer Mrs Stowe on behalf of the firm a percentage of the profits, and also a set of electrotype plates used in the illustrated edition in the hopes of securing the sheets of her next volume in advance. Beeton accordingly crossed the Atlantic in the late summer of the same year, and had what the authoress herself described as several "agreeable interviews" with her. By this time, however, other English publishers were in the field; and one of these, named Thomas Bosworth, Mrs Stowe had already allowed to say that his was "the only authorised edition offering me a percentage of the profits accruing from the sales." She consequently refused to commit herself at first to any engagement, though she readily admitted the foresight which the firm of Clarke and Beeton had displayed in publishing her book in England. The following is an extract from a letter which she wrote to Beeton at the time:

BRUNSWICK,
Sept. 27 [1852]

Your firm have showed great skill, address and ability in bringing the work before the British public. You undertook

[1] For fuller details see Henry Vizetelly, *Glances back through Seventy Years* (1893), vol. i, pp. 358–361, and an interesting article by Frederick Greenwood in *The Tatler* December 4, 1901.

it as a speculation, and from the report you have given me of the number sold it has not proved an unprofitable one. You have sold very nearly as many as Mr Jewett,[1] and tho' your price has been less, yet as you have not been embarrassed with any percentage to the author your profits on the whole must have been nearly equal to his, which I know have not been inconsiderable. I speak of this matter freely, for when American publishers have helped themselves to so many English works I have felt that it was no more than just that English publishers should have the same advantage of American ones. While, therefore, I do not conceive that I have any *claim* on an English publisher for any of the profits of an uncopyrighted work, I must say on the other hand neither should they advance any claim on *me* for getting it up, etc. The success of the book is their reward. They do it as a speculation and they gain by it. I am satisfied, but I stand uncommitted to them for it.

"The rampant Mænad of Massachusetts," as the poet Swinburne called her, was glad to have the electrotype plates for use in the anti-slavery cause, though there was one of them to which she entertained a strong objection. Unfortunately in the English illustrated edition the design for the cover had been supplied from this plate. Mrs Stowe goes on to state the ground of her objections in the same letter:

It was my desire in this work as much as possible to avoid resting the question of slavery on the coarser bodily horrors which have constituted the staple of anti-slavery books before now. They may be necessary in the commencement of a cause to arouse attention, but they may be dwelt on too long and to the exclusion of what is more profitable.

[1] John P. Jewett, Mrs Stowe's Boston publisher, who secured the American book rights for a 10-per-cent. royalty.

Hence you will observe that there is not one scene of bodily torture *described* in the book—they are *purposely* omitted. My object was to make more prominent those thousand worse tortures which slavery inflicts on the *soul*—the anguish of broken family ties, the suppression of the intellectual faculties, the religious persecution which it allows and legalises. It was therefore directly in opposition to the spirit of my intention to have a whipping scene on the very cover, and were I at liberty to authorize the work the plates of this kind would be to my mind an objection.

Though at first wishing to remain, as she put it, "unembarrassed by any engagements," Mrs Stowe eventually accepted £500 from Samuel Beeton, not admitting it as her share in the profits of the English editions, but as a voluntary gift from Clarke, Beeton, and Co. gratefully received. This sum was subsequently increased by £250 when he got back to England. In return she promised that Beeton's firm should bring out in conjunction with Bosworth and Sampson Low, the two other publishing houses which had profited most from her book, the so-called *Key to Uncle Tom's Cabin*, then in preparation and containing "all the original facts, anecdotes, and documents on which the story is founded, with some very interesting and affecting stories parallel to those told of Uncle Tom." As a souvenir of his visit to Brunswick she presented the youthful publisher with a large oil painting of "Uncle Tom and Little Eva" done on wood. Finally she gave Beeton introductions to various people, including the Secretary of the Anti-slavery Society, and her brother, the Rev. H. W. Beecher, the well-known Brooklyn preacher. The letter which she wrote to her brother is characteristic:

Dear Brother,

This will introduce to you Mr S. O. Beeton of the firm of Ch. Clarke and Co., London, publishers of several editions of my books. You will, I think, find pleasure in his conversation.

Yours,

H. B. STOWE

While in the United States Beeton was also able to visit Philadelphia and Boston, and to make the acquaintance of Longfellow, Oliver Wendell Holmes, Lowell, and other leaders of American literature. In the succeeding years he was to do much to introduce their works to English readers. He particularly appreciated the rich fund of humour which he found in the writings of such men as Artemus Ward and Mark Twain, and in bringing these as well before the English public he is worthy of our gratitude. But among his publications from American authors *Uncle Tom* remained by far his greatest success. He always hoped to relate the story of its publication himself, and on one occasion actually announced its forthcoming appearance; but for some reason the intention was never fulfilled.[1] By the spring of 1853 upward of a million copies had been issued from the presses of a dozen publishing houses in England. If many readers like Macaulay found it "a powerful and disagreeable book" they also agreed at the time with the distinguished Whig historian, albeit reluctantly, that on the whole it was "the most valuable addition that America has made to English literature."

[1] It was announced in *The Englishwoman's Domestic Magazine* (December 1869), but it never appeared.

III

The month which first saw the publication of *Uncle Tom's Cabin* under the imprint of Clarke, Beeton, and Co. also witnessed the issue from the same house of the first number of a new monthly magazine. This was *The Englishwoman's Domestic Magazine*, and it was among the first of its kind exclusively devoted to the female sex and its interests. Its price was twopence, so that it was within the reach of the pockets of all for whom it was intended. It owed its origin to S. O. Beeton, and was edited from the beginning by him. When it is remembered that Beeton spent the late summer and autumn of 1852 in America, and must have been away from England for more than two months, it must be admitted that the organization and conduct of the magazine during such a comparatively lengthy absence was a remarkable achievement on the part of a young man who was barely twenty-one.

The object of this new departure in journalism was stated by the editor in the first issue:

> *The Englishwoman's Domestic Magazine* will doubtless be found an encouraging friend to those of our countrywomen already initiated in the secret of making "home happy"; and to the uninitiated, who sometimes from carelessness but oftener from want of a guiding monitor have failed in this great particular, we shall offer hints and advice by which they may overcome every difficulty and acquire the art of rendering their efforts successful and their homes attractive.

It was therefore proposed to introduce such subjects as household management, cookery receipts, the toilette, dressmaking, gardening, "household pets," literary criticism, and fiction; and the approval with which they were received by the female public made them all permanent features in the magazine. In short, the editor's object was "to produce a work which should tend to the improvement of the intellect, the cultivation of the morals, and the cherishing of domestic virtues." Every effort, however, was made to avoid the appearance of being priggish and pedantic. "In carrying out this object," Beeton remarked when the magazine had been going for a year, "we have endeavoured to adopt a tone of morality free from severity, and to blend amusement with instruction."

The success of this woman's magazine surpassed the publisher's expectations. The circulation went up rapidly, and by the end of the second year it was 25,000. In the following year, in spite of the Crimean War, the paper gained 2000 fresh readers. In 1856 the circulation had risen to 37,000 and it continued to rise in the next few years. By 1860, the year which brought the first series to an end, the 50,000 mark had been reached, and the magazine was firmly established. At this time its pages were being illustrated by such well-known wood-cut artists as Henry Leech, Birket Foster, and Harrison Weir, while the editor's wife was contributing the notes on household management and cookery which formed the basis of her famous book.

The periodical owed much of its success to an entirely novel feature which was Beeton's idea. This was the introduction into the section known as "Our Practical Dress Instructor" of paper patterns which could be cut out by interested readers and greatly facilitated dressmaking in accordance with the latest fashions, the purpose being, as the editor put it, "that of inducing those who have time and opportunity to study the cultivation of dress in its most useful and becoming form." Beeton hoped that the directions accompanying the "working diagrams of the separate pieces, which form the whole pattern," would prove "so simple and easy that any lady may readily furnish herself with a paper pattern from them."[1]

Another feature proving a great attraction was the "Prize Composition," which Beeton quickly realized was one of the surest means of popularizing the magazine, as well as raising "the intellectual character of your young country-women by inducing them to venture into print." Both these novelties were eagerly seized upon by enterprising editors of other journals in due course, and the latter must be regarded as the forerunner of modern and highly successful newspaper competition. The subjects for which prizes were offered during the first year of *The Englishwoman's Domestic Magazine* were "The Duke of Wellington's Funeral," "On the Influence of a Mother's Teaching in After-life," and "Christmas Day in England, its Observances and Customs." A good start was made with upward of a hundred fair competitors for each prize. This attraction caught on, and at the same time the subjects became more intimate and controversial. In the two succeeding years, for instance, they included such themes as "The Unselfish Love of Woman contrasted with the Exacting Selfishness of Man" and "Do Married Rakes make the Best Husbands?"

One other novel feature may be mentioned here as achieving considerable popularity and being embodied in most subsequent women's journals. This was the column

[1] The first patterns were for "A Lady's Jacket and Vest," and they appeared in the first number of *The Englishwoman's Domestic Magazine* (May 1852), at pp. 17–19.

known as "Cupid's Letter Bag," in which the younger readers were invited to confide their troubles of the heart. The editor took upon himself the task of answering these delicate queries. The two following examples, which are selected at random from the earliest numbers, show that the lapse of nearly a century has made little difference to such readers and their problems. "Mary Ellis" writes from Knightsbridge:

I have had a quarrel with my lover, and the cause of it was my remarking rather sharply that while walking with him he could not pass a young lady in the street without looking tenderly at her. Since that evening he has not been to see me. Would there be any impropriety in my making advances towards effecting a reconciliation?

The editor's reply was a model of good advice:

We fear that the remark made by Mary to her lover was made in such a tone as to convey a notion of the termagant. Xantippe's is a character no man has a liking for. Employ some mutual friend to effect a reconciliation, and for the future remember Dean Swift's advice: "A woman may knit her stockings, but not her brow; curl her hair, but not her lips; use her tongue for persuasion, but not for scolding."

Again, "Laura S." writes from Hampton Court:

I am being constantly scolded by a maiden aunt for showing a preference for the society of two gentlemen at the same time. I assure you there can be no harm in it; for, as I flirt with both, neither can accuse me of showing a preference. Is it wrong, think you, to laugh and joke with an agreeable young man or two when you are not engaged?

Here the editorial warning was apt, and one hopes it was acted upon:

Laura, beware! Cupid cannot countenance such coquetry. Make your decision and be steadfast in your love. You will do well to remember that a coquette is a rose from which every lover plucks a leaf; the thorns are left for her future husband.

Finally, under the heading of fiction many stories appeared in this magazine, some complete in one issue and others which ran serially through several numbers. In the very first, for instance, was published the touching chapter on the slave sale from *Uncle Tom*. In the issue for October 1855 there appeared for the first time in England Edgar Allan Poe's famous short story "A Manuscript found in a Bottle." Two years later the editor, at the risk of considerable criticism, ran Nathaniel Hawthorne's celebrated tale of Puritan America, *The Scarlet Letter*, serially through twelve numbers. As powerful and disagreeable a romance in its own way as was *Uncle Tom*, Hawthorne's work had hitherto been placed among the books forbidden in most families to the "young person." Beeton disagreed with this view, and made up his mind that the readers of *The Englishwoman's Domestic Magazine* were sufficiently "emancipated" to read the book with understanding and sympathy. The subsequent rapid increase in the magazine's circulation would seem to have justified his judgment.

Encouraged by the success of *The Englishwoman's Domestic Magazine*, and being provided with all the capital he required for new ventures from the profits of *Uncle Tom*, which was still selling well, Beeton conceived the idea of starting a similar magazine for boys. His ambition, as he confessed some years later, was "to be regarded as having founded a periodical literature for the young folk of our country, such as exists in no other land, sail you East or

D

West." Surely there are few more laudable ambitions than this? "I can hardly imagine a more responsible task for a man," he said,

> than the undertaking to answer for the matter and manner of literature intended for the youth of one's country. No small thing I count it to help to form the taste and influence the mind of a youth; whose glorious heritage it is to possess the Empire that their fathers have founded and preserved and whose duty it will be to hold that Empire, handing it down greater, more prosperous, to future generations.

The work which Beeton had in mind and which led the way for many other boys' publications with which he was connected was *The Boy's Own Magazine*. Its first number came out in January 1855; and, as the lack of suitable reading for boys in attractive form had long been felt, it was an immediate success.

The new periodical appeared at the same price and in the same form as *The Englishwoman's Domestic Magazine*, and, like it, was also a monthly. Striking an entirely fresh note, it was among the first of its kind to cater exclusively for this particular class of reader. Features such as the "Prize Composition" which had been popular in the women's journal and could be adapted to the new venture were utilized with effect. Boys who submitted winning contributions on subjects like "True Courage," "The Buccaneers and their Exploits," and "Sir Charles James Napier's Indian Victories" received a silver pencil-case value a guinea. Another feature, more directly designed to promote sales of this magazine, was a ballot among purchasers of each issue for prizes consisting of gold chains, silver lever watches, and other jewellery. Such a proceeding would probably be illegal to-day under the

betting and lottery legislation. In the words of its sub-
title, *The Boy's Own Magazine* was "an illustrated Journal
of Fact, Fiction, History and Adventure." Besides bio-
graphies of Dick Whittington, James Watt, Captain Cook,
Christopher Columbus, and other "boys who have become
great men," there were adventures with boa-constrictors,
buffaloes, bears, wolves, eagles, "and other denizens of the
Forest and the Prairie, copiously illustrated with characteristic engravings." In addition, there were sections devoted
to topography, nature study, popular science, and sports
and pastimes. The early contributors included Captain
Mayne Reid, W. H. Davenport Adams, W. B. Rands,
J. G. Edgar, the younger Thomas Hood, and James
Greenwood.

It was a remarkable band of young men whose stories
and articles enriched the pages of the new magazine.
Mayne Reid was an Ulsterman who had emigrated as a
youth to America, where he had led a most adventurous
life and had seen service with the United States forces in
the Mexican War. He had recently returned to England,
and had begun to turn out the first in a long succession of
romances for boys, such as *The Rifle Rangers* and *The Scalp
Hunters*, which were to run serially in *The Boy's Own
Magazine*. Davenport Adams contributed material later
published as *Memorable Battles in English History*, *Famous
Regiments*, and *Famous Ships of the British Navy*. W. B.
Rands was a reporter in the Press Gallery of the House of
Commons. When Parliament was not sitting he sent
Beeton verse as well as prose, being well dubbed "the
laureate of the nursery." J. G. Edgar came from Berwick-
shire, and had spent his early years working for a business
firm in the West Indies. His first book, *The Boyhood of*

Great Men, was written for Beeton's latest periodical. He had a remarkable knowledge of the border tradition in English and Scottish history, which he used with great effect in his historical books for boys.

Then there was Tom Hood, the comic poet and caricaturist, later editor of *Fun.* He was responsible for some lively "pen and pencil pictures," though his best novel, *Captain Master's Children,* was written for the sister publication, *The Englishwoman's Domestic Magazine.* Finally there was James Greenwood, a pioneer of the boy's club movement, who invented the phrase "working boy." Greenwood, who depicted life among lower-class boys at this time, was something of a rough diamond: a younger brother of Frederick Greenwood, first editor of the *Pall Mall Gazette,* he was to astonish London a decade later with his work *The Amateur Casual,* which was published in his brother's journal and described life in the workhouses of the metropolis. James Greenwood was only a year younger than Samuel Beeton, and must have had a remarkable constitution to stand up to the Bohemian life he led for so long, for he was destined to survive the First World War and to die in 1929, at the age of ninety-seven.

The story of the rapid success of the enterprise is best told in the editor's own words in the preface to the first annual volume:

As for books for general reading, we could not remember one suited to the tastes and requirements of a boy. Thereupon we at once set about the establishment of the *Boy's Own Magazine* and number one appeared. "This won't do," we heard on all sides. "It is too *high,* too *solid,* too *good.*" They were not boys who said so, and we waited till we heard what would be said by the boys. We waited to know whether books written in words of one syllable were *always* to be the companions of youth; or whether it had not also advanced with all the advancement about us, and was fit for stronger meat than the Goody Two Shoes style of composition. Well, a few months decided the question, and our readers instead of remaining a few, as was predicted, increased by thousands, and went on increasing. We then pitched the tone of the Magazine a little higher; and more Boys—more thousands of Boys—rushed to buy. The experiment succeeded.

Other periodicals fashioned on similar lines were not slow to follow in the wake of the pioneer. One of these entitled the *Youth's Instructor* went so far as to embody in its first issue the "prize composition" plan and much of the prospectus of *The Boy's Own Magazine*. However, as Beeton was happy to relate, "it was found impossible to produce at the price so good a magazine as the *Boy's Own*," and the result was that Beeton eventually took over the *Youth's Instructor* and incorporated it in his own journal. Though it never quite reached the circulation enjoyed by *The Englishwoman's Domestic Magazine*, the *Boy's Own* could boast of youthful readers to the number of 40,000 in 1862, the year in which the first series came to an end. Furthermore, S. O. Beeton always regarded it as his favourite publication. "It is that which above all our little possessions we look upon with the greatest affection," he admitted after the magazine had been going some years. There was no doubt now in which direction his particular genius lay. Among those who saw this was his young wife, who became engaged to him in the year the *Boy's Own* was started, and who wrote to him characteristically at the time:

I do sincerely hope and trust that Beeton's *Boy's* will
answer your expectations in every way; I have not the
slightest fear that it will for, if you choose, you may do
anything you like either with boys or girls.

IV

It is worth while glancing for a few moments at Clarke,
Beeton, and Co.'s current list of publications. First of
all there were the two magazines which were the junior
partner's particular pride and interest. Next, under the
heading of "Literature for the Rail," came sundry items
both instructive and diverting, which cost a shilling each.
They varied from *Select Scenes from Shakespeare* to *How to
get Money* and *Emigrant's Guide to Australia*. Then there
was the "Readable Books" series, which had been taken
over from Henry Vizetelly, and which was described as
"a Library, suited as regards Price to the Purse, and as
regards Portability to the Pocket." Works in this series,
which were priced at one and six in cloth and a shilling in
wrappers, included Southey's *Life of Nelson*; similar studies
of Wellington and Napoleon; *The Guards, or The Household Troops of England*, by Captain Rafter; Edgar Allan
Poe's *Tales of Mystery, Imagination and Humour*; a book by
another American writer, Ik Marvel, entitled *Reveries of a
Bachelor*; and, possibly designed as a companion to the
preceding volume, *Philosophers and Actresses: Scenes, Vivid
and Picturesque, from the Hundred and One Dramas of Art and
Passion*, by Arsène Houssaye. Few readers, we learn from
the contents page of this work, "will require to be informed that the following pages are translated from the
French." This surprising publication, needless to add, had
been originally chosen by Vizetelly, who was inclined to

the Gallic way of life. It contrasts strangely with the
"Select Series of Gift Books for the Sons and Daughters
of England," also published by Clarke, Beeton, which
contained such admirable moral productions as *The
Gambler's Wife*, by Miss Pickering, *The Tell-tale, or Sketches
of Domestic Life in the United States*, and, of course, the
American Elizabeth Wetherell's celebrated novel *The
Wide, Wide World*. This last enjoyed an outstanding
success, although many of those who were obliged by
their parents to read it must have agreed with Lord
Frederick Hamilton's description of it as a tale about "a
tiresome little girl named Ellen Montgomery, who apparently divided her time between reading her pocket Bible
and indulging in paroxysms of tears."

As might be expected, there were several works in the
list on the subject of Negro slavery, in addition to Mrs
Beecher Stowe's immortal contribution. They included
Slavery Poems, by Longfellow, Southey, and Whittier.
There was also a book by another American, R. Hildreth,
called *The White Slave*, which, contrary to the suggestion
implied in its title, did not deal with the traffic reputed to
flourish in Buenos Aires. It did, however, contain another
whipping scene on the cover—this time of a woman
stripped to the waist—which no doubt stimulated sales, but
must have sent Mrs Beecher Stowe into an explosion of
righteous wrath, had she chanced to see it. Naturally there
were various editions of *Uncle Tom*, ranging from a paper-
back with no illustrations which cost sixpence to a strik-
ingly handsome version "beautifully printed and splendidly
illustrated with engravings by the first Artists, forming a
Series of Pictorial Shames [*sic*] against the Crime of
Slavery." This edition sold for seven and six, and its pur-

chasers had the further satisfaction of knowing that "these Pictorial Illustrations are executed in a style which has never been surpassed in the history of printing." The scene to which Mrs Beecher Stowe objected so strongly was actually embossed in gold on the cover of this edition. Finally, for particularly ardent admirers of Mrs Stowe and her works there were lithograph portraits of the authoress herself, which could be had from the offices in Fleet Street for as little as five shillings.

It will be remembered that before Beeton left the United States in the autumn of 1852 he obtained from Mrs Stowe a promise of the early sheets of her next volume, *The Key to Uncle Tom's Cabin*. In conjunction with the two other publishers already mentioned, Beeton undertook to secure for it the protection of English copyright law, so that when the book appeared it could not be 'pirated,' as *Uncle Tom* had so widely been. The purpose of this work lay in the numerous attacks on *Uncle Tom* in which the authenticity of many of the incidents recounted there had been questioned by the slave-owners. The authoress was, therefore, induced to prepare, as she put it, a key to unlock *Uncle Tom's Cabin*, which would present "the original facts and documents upon which the story is founded, together with corroborative statements verifying the truth of the work." The characters in *Uncle Tom* were carefully analysed in the *Key*, and some indication was given of the originals on which they were modelled; the question of the treatment of the slaves was examined, and many cases of brutality quoted from State trials and other documents; and the legal and social aspects of slavery were discussed.

To the workers in the anti-slavery cause in America the *Key* rendered considerable service, but, whatever its value as political propaganda in the United States, the wisdom of reprinting it in large quantities in England was very doubtful. It had been agreed that the original edition should be published under the joint imprint of Sampson Low, Son, and Co., Clarke, Beeton, and Co., and Thomas Bosworth, and that subsequently each of these three houses would be free to reprint as many copies as they liked in cheap editions. It is not clear how strongly the reprint was advocated by Beeton, but the fact remains that a large edition was brought out by the firm in 1853, 50,000 copies according to Henry Vizetelly, who adds that the greater part of it fell like a drug on the market. It is said that this publication involved Clarke and Beeton in heavy losses; at all events, Clarke's father, who had gone security for him, declined to put up any more capital, and so the partnership was eventually dissolved.

When Clarke and Beeton parted company early in 1855 it was agreed that Beeton should acquire the sole copyright in *The Englishwoman's Domestic Magazine* and *The Boy's Own Magazine*, both of which he was anxious to edit and publish on his own account. These and Beeton's other publications were now issued from 18 Bouverie Street, where he took offices. Here he remained till 1860, when he moved into more spacious premises at 248 Strand, on the site of the present Law Courts. For the time being he continued his association with Salisbury, who had his printing works in Bouverie Street.

Chapter III

COURTSHIP AND MARRIAGE

IT WAS towards the middle of the year 1855 that S. O. Beeton became engaged to be married. His fiancée was Isabella Mayson, an attractive and good-looking girl of nineteen with brown hair, who had recently returned from school in Germany. At this time, as we have seen, she was living at Epsom with her mother and stepfather, Henry Dorling, the printer of the Epsom race-cards and lessee of the Grand Stand.

Isabella Mary Mayson was born on March 14, 1836, at her father's house in Milk Street, in the City of London, in the same street in which Samuel Beeton had spent his childhood. Her parents had been married in the previous year, and she was their first child.

Since they were neighbours in Milk Street, it is likely that Mr and Mrs Benjamin Mayson and the Powell Beetons were on friendly terms; it is practically certain that Benjamin Mayson and his wife were customers of The Dolphin. When Elizabeth Mayson married Henry Dorling some years later she did not forget her old friends in Milk Street, and it is significant that she should have sent her daughter Bella to the same finishing school in Heidelberg where two of Sam Beeton's younger sisters were pupils. Sam and Bella had probably played together as children in the Milk Street days; it is probable that he met her again when she was home on holiday from Germany.

At Heidelberg Isabella learned, among other accomplishments, to speak French and German fluently. The headmistress noticed with approval her interest in cooking, and some years later, when she was preparing her famous *Book of Household Management*, this good *Hausfrau* sent her a volume of German recipes, many of which were used in the first edition of the work. On her return to England Isabella found time from her arduous domestic duties to keep up her interest in languages by reading the latest French and German books as they appeared. She also practised pastry-making with the local confectioner in Epsom. This latter conduct, according to her sister's testimony, "was supposed to be ultra modern and not quite nice!" She developed a talent for music, and used to go up to London regularly to take lessons on the pianoforte with Sir Julius Benedict.

Sam proposed to Isabella about the time of the Spring Meeting in 1855. The favourite for the Derby that year was Wild Dayrell, whose trainer, Robert Sherwood, was a great friend of the Dorling family. Although the scandals connected with Epsom racing in the forties belonged to the past, abuses still occurred: concerted attempts were made by a gang, for instance, to 'nobble' the favourite for the big race. Fortunately, owing to the trainer's vigilance, the attempts were unsuccessful—evidence of interference with the horse's travelling-box was discovered just in time to avert a serious accident—and Wild Dayrell duly romped home at even money. To mark the occasion Sherwood gave Isabella Mayson a rich dress-length of red-striped silk. It was in the dress made from this material that she shortly afterwards posed for the daguerreotype picture which now hangs in the National Portrait Gallery, and which has been reproduced as the frontispiece to this book.

Isabella's engagement to Beeton seems to have encountered a good deal of opposition at first on the part of her parents and relatives. This was no doubt due to the feeling that, though he had created a certain stir in the publishing world, he was by no means securely established in his business calling. Then, too, there were the usual lovers' quarrels which must at times have jeopardized the prospects of marriage. But perhaps that was to be expected, for the course of true love never runs quite smooth. Both were young, and, fortified rather than hindered by their youth, they made up their minds from the outset to triumph over the difficulties which confronted them. The brief correspondence which passed between them during this trying period shows to some extent how they succeeded.

The first letter is from Isabella, and was written in answer to an invitation from her fiancé to hear the great Swedish soprano Jenny Lind sing at a concert.

EPSOM,
Decbr. 26th, —55

MY DEAREST SAM,

Your kind letter I did not receive till this morning, so of course was unable to answer it before. I trust however this will reach you in time. I do not know how to thank you enough for your kind invitation, the more delightful because so unexpected; to hear Jenny Lind again was a treat I never anticipated, so if you come down to-night I shall be quite ready to go back with you tomorrow.

Walter I am happy to say is much better, as also the other children on the Hill. Frank is progressing towards recovery, but still wants a deal of nursing, and this morning Lucy has just made up her mind to be ill, so you may imagine we are not in a very healthy condition taking us all together.

I cannot say I spent a happy Christmas day, *you* can well guess the reason and besides that Frank being so poorly, we were not in spirits to enjoy ourselves. I should very much have liked to have sent you as long a letter as you sent me but Frank is impatient to be dressed, and you know invalids are not the most patient people in the world.

Hoping to see you this evening as soon as you can, with best love,

Believe me, dearest Sam,

Yours most affectionately,

ISABELLA

The "children on the Hill," Walter, Frank, and Lucy, were her step-brothers and -sisters, whom she helped to look after in the Grand Stand on the Epsom Race-course.

Isabella enjoyed the concert, though, as she subsequently confessed, she was afraid her Sam was going to be "seriously ill" when they parted. He had had a distressing and ominous fit of coughing. "Mind and take proper care of yourself, as you promised me you would," she said in her next letter. Such injunctions as these were unfortunately not always heeded, for young Samuel Beeton was a glutton for work, and the shadow of ill-health had already begun to darken his life. From his mother he had inherited a tendency towards consumption, that grim scourge of so many families of the time, and there were already indications such as fits of coughing that the disease was getting a grip on him and undermining his physique. The wonder is that he managed to get through so much work as he did, for at times he must have suffered terribly.

On January 3, 1856, she wrote again from Epsom:

I cannot say I read your note with any degree of satis-faction, it was so full of the miserables. I was indeed sorry to hear you had been such a sufferer; now your enemy has departed you will be able to enjoy yourself in the country, and come back looking as jolly as a fat farmer. You know very well how I should like you to appear on your return. I intended writing to invite you to join our family circle on Saturday, as we are going to the Stand to keep Christmas now the small ones are recovered. I see however by your note that we are not to have the pleasure of your Company. I am not disappointed in one respect, for I think change of air and Suffolk living will do you more good than romping with the children. . . .

In this letter Isabella enclosed some plain envelopes: the reason was that Sam had been writing to her from his office in Bouverie Street, using envelopes embossed with the design of *The Boy's Own Magazine*. This had not gone unnoticed by Papa Dorling:

I hope you will not be offended with me for sending you a few envelopes. Father said this morning [that] he supposed your passion for advertising was such that you could not resist sending those stamped affairs. Pray do not think me rude, but I cannot bear for all the world to know who my letter comes from.

Samuel Beeton went down to Suffolk as he had planned, much to the relief of his fiancée, who thought he "really looked very queer" before he left. During his stay there she sent him an account of her doings by nearly every post:

We spent a very merry evening at the Stand on Saturday. I was very sorry you were not present, for I am sure you would have enjoyed yourself. We kept it up till midnight as late as we possibly could, considering it was just upon Sunday morning.

She even tried to tempt him to cut short his visit and return for a family dinner with her parents at Epsom:

I hope you will not disappoint me because you know very well these formal feeds I abominate, and if you come of course it will be much pleasanter for me. I am the only one of the girls going to dine with them, so pray do not leave me to sit for three or four hours with some old man I do not care a straw about.

Meanwhile two of Sam's step-sisters, Eliza and Victoria, who had been staying with the Dorlings in Epsom, suggested a trip to town for another concert:

Your sisters have kindly invited me to come up with them on Friday to the Concert, but as you said nothing about it on Sunday to *me*, I thought I would write and ascertain your intentions on the subject, as if you will not object to letting me know about it I shall feel much obliged.

You went off in such a hurry the other morning, I have scarcely recovered the shock yet. Your reason for so doing I suppose was business. Before this you will have received an invitation from Mr White[1] for the 6th. I am very sorry you will not be able to go, for I think you would enjoy yourself.

Your sisters are dragging on a miserable existence here, doing plenty of embroidery and going out for gigantic walks and coming home covered in mud. I am afraid they must feel it rather dull. . . .

[1] Jane, one of Henry Dorling's daughters by his first wife, had married a solicitor named White.

In reply to this letter Sam made a reference to difficulties
with his prospective parents-in-law:

LONDON
Jany 31, 1856

MY DEAR BELLA,

I am very delighted to think I am going to see you to-
morrow, and can only say that I consider I owe a large debt
of gratitude to my sisters, in prevailing on you to come to
London, to Sig. Opertz's concert: the suggestions of your
most humble and loving servant have been latterly so unfortunately received that I have not had the courage to utter
my notions with respect to your going anywhere or doing
anything. I had *heard* nothing decidedly and distinctly from
any quarter on the concert subject, and that was the simple
reason why *I said* nothing to you about it on Sunday. You
write "you say," to ascertain my intentions—they are on
this point as they always are on every matter connected
with you, (whom I prize and love beyond all others and all
other things) to do precisely and exactly as you wish. It will
gratify me greatly to see you tomorrow, and if you can
find means to let me know by what train you will arrive in
town, I will meet you at London Bridge.

Mr White's very kind, informal invitation reached me
here this morning. I shall reply to it, after I have finished
my devoir to you, and I undoubtedly feel very vexed not to
be able to be there—you will enjoy yourself, very much, I
hope, and find some good partners. . . .

. . . tonight I go again to Perkes' Manor House Hotel—
I like immensely the walk up to and from town morning
and evening, with cold bath before a good breakfast. If
you can come up, dear Bella, to-morrow in time to go for
a short walk with me, I should be very glad, and if I can't
hear from Epsom what time you will come to town, tell
them at Milk St to send down to Bouverie, the moment

you are there, and on the wings of—but I had forgotten—no
namby pamby nonsense, so dearest Bella, I am,

Yours with fondest love,

S. O. BEETON

II

Samuel Beeton had been looking round for a suitable
house to make their future home. The choice was finally
made a dozen or so miles away at Pinner. The Wood-
ridings estate was at this time being developed for building,
and a pair of semi-detached red-brick houses known as
Chandos Villas had been completed a few months previously on the Uxbridge Road. They had a fifty-foot
frontage and a depth of 250 feet, and they were let at a
rental of £50 a year. As an attraction to the inhabitants of
this new suburb, which was then quite a small hamlet, the
estate agents undertook to provide each tenant with a
season ticket on the railway for seven years. This consideration seems to have outweighed the ugliness of the
house, as Sam signed the lease of No. 2 Chandos Villas and
collected his season ticket.[1]

Most of his subsequent letters during the engagement
tell of the arrangements as to furniture, the garden, and so
on which were being put in hand there:

Yes, I've been to *Pinner* once or twice this week [he wrote
on April 6]; *our gardeners* have levelled the garden, and
commenced digging the borders.

To this progress report Isabella replied:

. . . I think you are getting on famously with your opera-
tions at Pinner. I shall scarcely know the place when I go

[1] In September 1940 Chandos Villas suffered a direct hit through enemy action,
and were completely destroyed.

E

down next. You wished to know my favorite seeds; I have no partiality for anything particular but Mignonette, and I think that would look best planted at the edge of the border; however, please yourself and you please me, my dear. Honeysuckle, Jasmine, Clematis, Canaryanthus, are all very pretty creepers. The first-named grows very quickly and soon covers a place, and that I think is very desirable at Pinner. Our garden begins to look quite green; it is capital growing weather.

This crossed another letter from Sam written on the same day, Sunday, on his return to Fleet Street. It begins with a typical Victorian pun, of the kind which abound in the pages of *Punch* of the period:

I commenced the day badly I fear, for I was *violating* the Sabbath by *violetting* in the fields and roads, this morning round Pinner. Fred P.[1] went down with me last night, and we "made out," as the Yankees say, tolerably. I had excessively interesting interviews with the band of Pinner tradesmen and handicraftsmen—your bricklayer commenced making the place in a mess on Tuesday morning, your carpenter commences his cupboards on the same day, and your painter follows them up closely at the end of the week.

Mr Cutbush, the Nursery*man*—not woman—of your establishment is going to run down to Pinner to-morrow afternoon to see what Shrubs, Creepers, etc. are the best to plant. I have to go and choose the Chimney Piece to-morrow—I do heartily wish you were here to go with me —I've no doubt I shall make a terrible mess over this and other matters. What colour are your Venetian Blinds to be? *Green* or *Drab*? They will have to be made, I apprehend— Do your parents know any good man? Messrs Green and Co., Baker St, you can purchase some furniture of, if you

<hr>

[1] His stepbrother, F. P. Beeton.

like. I have £120-worth to come from there, as per agreement—Will you ask your Mama if she knows them—from all I can learn, they are first-rate people.

Our bachelor bedroom is quite comfy—the bed and bedstead are capital, and the chest of drawers, complete with toilet cover, with my old Buffalo rug before the fire-place and a washing stand, borrowed from Mrs Scott constitute the furniture—I had forgotten—the sheet nailed in front of the window, so as not to expose us too much to Mrs Brown's ken[1]—We took down Coffee, and Sugar and Sausages, and had a good tea last night, and a first-rate breakfast this morning—went last night to Pinner Village, which was quite in commotion, being Saturday—I really believe I saw 10 people altogether. The Butcher's shop near the Church was driving a tremendous trade, and vice versa; this morning the Church was doing all the business.

Sam's next letter tells how business is booming and how he proposed to spend a Saturday afternoon at the Crystal Palace. Isabella writes back enthusiastically falling in with his arrangements, but confessing, as she frequently does in her letters to him, her doubts as to whether she is really worthy of his love. The Crystal Palace, it may be noted here, was a great feature in the metropolitan life of the fifties and sixties. Originally designed by Sir Joseph Paxton for the Great Exhibition in Hyde Park in 1851, it had now been transferred a year or two later to the site which it occupied at Sydenham until it was accidentally destroyed by fire in 1936. Its fountains and artificial lakes and grottos were long a favourite resort of Londoners and others who could snatch "a day off" from the common task.

[1] His neighbour, who lived at No. 1 Chandos Villas.

[*April* 23]

My beloved Bella,

I have, how-ever, a very good case now to lay before your Royal vision—next Saturday, April 26, is the last Saturday available for your Crystal Palace Ticket, so does it not appear unto thy judgment (without appealing to any softer feeling) that to the C.P. you and I should go? . . .

Now then, business, and no more nonsense! Attention! Shoulder, etc. Sweet peas, Mignonette, and Honeysuckle ordered, and arranged for—Wine Cellar, ditto—Scarlet Runners, also—I have been hoping for Rain this evening, but it hasn't come down yet, looks very much like it, still, and which it would do the turf much good if it would but come—yes! (sic Scott) Silver Spoons not prigged yet! Cupboard under Cellar commenced—how the shelves are to be fixed, can't at all see. Perhaps you will oblige me with a Crayon sketch. . . .

From another arrangement into which I have entered with Messrs Green and Co. you will have, or can have, nearly two hundred pounds worth of Furniture—as soon as you please—what a rash, reckless character, I am, am I not? Lamps not come, whereat I am wroth, that is, irritable! I think, with your good and kind assistance I shall be able to overcome that foe of yours and mine, which you have charitably dubbed irritability.

Again to the house reverting, the Kitchen's painted and the Grate is properly fixed, so as to be useful in case of much fire being required for our "petit-diners."

Isabella's reply came by return, although the post at Pinner was not quick enough for her liking:

Of course I shall be delighted to accompany you to the Crystal Palace and will be on Anerley Bridge at 1.30 by the same train I came up before, tomorrow afternoon (Saturday) and will wait for you there.

They do not seem to be particularly quick in postal arrangements at Pinner, for I did not receive your note till this morning. How do you account for it?

I fancy I could draw a plan for shelves in that cupboard you were speaking of, but as it would be absolutely necessary for me to be on the spot to explain the said plan, I think I had better bring it up with me to-morrow.

Many thanks also for having the mignonette sown; you will, I am sure, quite spoil me, you attend so to my smallest wishes and desires.

Do not be too sanguine, dear Sam, do not look forward to too much happiness for fear of being disappointed in *me*. It is the only thing I fear; that however remains to be proved, whether my fears are groundless or no. I think they may prove so. . . .

Sam had been inclined to doubt whether his intended would be able to guide herself when removed from parental control and "left to her own exertions." These letters show how the two lovers resolved their difficulty:

EPSOM,
May 26th—56

As I have here two or three little matters in your note of yesterday which rather puzzled me, I thought I must write and ask an explanation. . . .

In the first place in what does Bella *sometimes now* pain Sam just a little? Why does he not wish to be near her? Secondly; what right has he to conjure up in his fertile imagination any such nasty things as rough corners to smooth down, when there is one who loves him better and more fondly than ever one human being did another on *this* earth at least.

Oh, Sam, I think it is so wrong of you to fancy such dreadful things. You say also you don't think I shall be able to guide myself when I am left to my own exertions. I must certainly say I have always looked up to, and respected both parents and perhaps have been *too* mindful of what they say (I mean respecting certain matters), but then in a very short time you will have the entire management of me and I can assure you that you will find in me a most docile and yielding pupil.

Pray don't imagine when I am yours—that things will continue the same as they are now. God forbid. Better would it be to put an end to this matter altogether if we thought there was the slightest probability of *that*, so pray don't tremble for our future happiness. Look at things in a more rosy point of view, and I have no doubt with the love *I am sure* there is existing between us we shall get on as merrily as crickets, with only an occasional sharp point to soften down, and not as many as you fancy. . . .

In return for her assurances, and in compensation for his scepticism, he invited her to see the grand firework display which was to be staged in celebration of the end of the Crimean War.

I have seen my Mother and Sisters to-day, on the question of the fireworks, which I am going seriously to attack. My Mother would have asked all of you to come to-morrow, and perambulate the streets in a huge van, but that she knew it would be impossible for you all to come —now as she and the girls say, can *you* not be spared for the day? What say you? I could even take you back to Epsom the same night, if such may be the rigid order.

These fireworks you ought to see, not so much as a sight, but as an epoch to be remembered, and talked of afterwards, in years to come,—all these great and marked spectacles I should exceedingly like my own dear Bella to see, for I do think they are most advantageous in many points of view, and especially in that denominated private view, which can be managed, malgré the van.

The date fixed for the wedding was now drawing near, and the happy pair lived in a world of bustle and excitement, bridesmaid's dresses, invitations to the guests, and the usual preparations for the event. The attitude of some of Isabella's relatives was still rather disconcerting, and in the midst of all this Sam was launching another boy's magazine.

BOUVERIE,
Sunday Evg. [*June 2*]

I received a visit from your Aunts Eliza and Jane, and yr. Uncle Ted yesterday, and was most pained to hear of the many disagreeables that have occurred during the races. All spoke most kindly, but I am very grieved that your Aunt Eliza won't come to the wedding next month—her principal motive in coming to the Office was to beg that neither you nor I should consider in any degree that it was a slight to us. Oh! how much happier would the dwellers in this world be if they thought a little more of others, and a little less of self. I hope, my dearest love, that you have not been bearing many cutting speeches during the last day or two. I fear that you are made very miserable oftentimes on my poor account—n'importe, a little more than a month, and I hope and think you will be a happy little wife— meanwhile let me know in what way I can *now* lighten your burden, and it shall be done.

Will you come up on Thursday, and choose the Bedstead, Furniture, and Kitchen Utensils? My Mother is going to Oxford, so if you think well, will you ask your Mamma if she will come with you to assist your selection. . . .

Your Toilet table, I have ordered, and the Carpenter and his bench will remove from Pinner to-morrow. Mrs Scott is to commence a thorough cleaning of the house from top to bottom—the dining room paper has arrived from Paris, and will be on the Walls I trust on Tuesday, and by the end of the Week I hope some of the goods and chattels— S.I.B.—will be in Chandos Villas. I have so much on my hands after to-morrow week that I should feel very grateful if your Mamma and you would assist in putting the finishing stroke on the furnishing details in conjunction with the Milk St. division.

> LONDON, BOUVERIE,
> *Friday aftn.*
> [*c. June 6*]

. . . touching upon that part of your note relative to the garden at Pinner, I have succeeded in purchasing at a low rate a quantity of loads of most astonishingly good "Brick Rubbish." This will do admirably for the paths. Mr Scott, demurring slightly to my suggestion, has built with some of the best of the bricks (for a lot of them are whole) an impromptu and rather primitive hot bed for a vegetable marrow plant which was presented to me yesterday, and an excessively imposing appearance it presents.

With respect to what you say about a Bath, another Cistern will be requisite in order to have water laid on up stairs, on 1st floor.

The Carpenter has finished your cupboard in the passage —and it's a grand place—there'll be room for four people to sleep if we're hard up for beds. The nice fresh smell of the wholesome paint, as you observed in a portion of your letter, still obtains as much as ever, only more so. I am told this will gradually increase until a most healthful climax is reached; I can only add I'm exceedingly grateful. The weather, as you imagined, has been bitterly cold, but then one doesn't feel it much, because there are no blinds to any of the windows, or carpets on the floor, and a lack of furniture to the beds—in addition to which I may name, as an extra advantage, the fact of the sashes and frames being in such order that they freely admit a very large amount of the chilly exterior atmosphere—and the doors are usually all widely open.

You are right in your supposition that we have been very busy in Bouverie St—and now, to lay aside irony, I have to tell you that I have now commenced preparations for launching the new Barque—"Beeton's Boy's Own Journal" —(so to be christened) and shall have, consequently, much on my hands until it is fairly before the public on Saturday, June 14. I am sanguine of success, and I *know* you would write me a line or two (be they never so short, or even scolding) if you had a notion, my dearest one, of the cheering influence, the fresh life, new vigour and increased strength which your most valued lines ever impart. The reason is simply this—I can think and work and do so much better and so much more when I can see and feel that it is not for myself, (about whom I care nothing) I am laboring, but for her whom I so ardently prize, so lovingly cherish in my inmost heart—my own Bella! I believe most surely in her truth and troth, and I do like to see the words written by her "My dear Sam."

I shall have so much to do to-morrow and on Sunday morning, prospectus writing, and arranging for the B.O.J. that I don't think I shall be able to see you this week. If I come, it will be on Sunday aftn., but don't expect me. . . .

The last letters before the wedding show how much the strain of the preceding weeks had told on Samuel Beeton, and how much he was looking forward to settling down with his bride in their home at Pinner after the brief honeymoon which they had planned to enjoy abroad.

LONDON, BOUVERIE,
Saturday Aftn
[*c. June* 14]

MY DEAREST BELLA,

As I cannot see you this evening, I do the best I can in default thereof, and write you a few lines. I have had a very hard day's work—indeed this week has been to me one of the most anxious I have ever passed—and after the excitement and bother, I feel quite used up. How much I should like to see you now, and nestling quietly beside you, forget all else, and, dreaming deliciously, have a notion that there existed nothing in the world beyond my loved Bella. The wear and tear of the past few months—happy as many, many hours have been—seem naught in comparison with the feverish impatience I now feel to be fairly through the next two or three weeks. How glad I shall be to get you to our quiet home at Pinner, after the race on the Continent, and commence in right good earnest a settled life, for which after all my wanderings and vagaries I yearn immensely.

The *Boy's Own Journal* has gone off pretty well—not quite so well as I had anticipated by Wednesday's sale—however, it promises exceedingly well and will require a longer nursing (that is all) than I had intended to have given it. My quality of obstinacy will have to be brought forth.

You are a very good, kind girl to invite me to Brighton, and I hope you won't think me a barbarian for not coming, but I have so many things to do which I can do on Sunday alone.

Tell me when you are coming to London next week, so that I may see you, and with all the love of which my heart is capable.

I am yours,

S. O. BEETON

PINNER,
Sunday Eveng
[*June* 17]

MY BELOVED BELLA,

I have been wandering through the fields, full of the newly cut hay, for the last hour or so, and have returned home perfectly envious and full of bile—for I assure you I was the only unhappy mortal who was alone. I met many happy maidens with many happy men, sometimes one male with two females; at other times the animal and panniers were reversed, but there was always somebody with somebody else, so to this fact do you owe, my dearest, this letter, as I have made up my mind to be even with the people I have seen in some way or other, and if they are *with* those they love, they cannot, at any rate, be experiencing this pleasure now felt by me of writing to her "in whose hands are all the corners of my heart."

You must have had a lovely day at Brighton, for here it has been charmingly sunshiny—the moon is electro-typing at this moment with its beautiful silvery light all around, and I instinctively am walking with you on Brighton pier, and almost hear you ejaculate "Oh! Sam, if you only knew." I don't know why it is, Bella mia, but you never get any further than that. But I am getting into Cabs again —am I not, darling? and I shall be leaving something again at the Opera, and be obliged, reluctantly, to return for it, and then, perhaps, you will be cross at my carelessness in leaving anything behind—but then it's so like the thoughtlessness of that chap Sam, you will reflect, and pardon me.

Now, down to Earth again, and let Furniture act on us as attention! on a regiment on parade. What colour are the Cord Tassels to be? These Blinds, Oh! these blinds, I can't get along with them at all. The Plumber and carpenter have departed the house at last—peace go with them!—

pieces they've left behind. The rooms are all cleaned—the stoves polished—I took the brushes down—quite ready for carpets and blinds, and all the rest of your property. I have written a note to your friend, Mr Green, that he can send down the food for Chandos as soon as he please, as it's quite ready to be lined. . . .

Bella dearest, 3 Sundays more, and then the Holidays, as school-phrase has it. It seems to me impossible. None can tell how grateful I feel and am to the "Great God," for having brought me thus near to a point of earthly felicity which, twelve little months ago, I dared not have hoped for. May He bless and protect you, my own dearest one, and make us happy, and contented in each other's true and ardent love. *Je t'embrasse de tout mon coeur.*

Yours in all things,
S. O. BEETON

Isabella on her side responded bravely, giving good counsel and some earnest of the loving kindness which she intended to bestow upon her future husband when they were united:

EPSOM,
Iune 20th, 1856

MY DEAREST SAM,

We were so busy yesterday we had no time to call upon you about the cards. I enclose you Mr Ward's and Haggerty's invitation, and must trouble you to forward them as we do not know their address. I hope to hear from you to-morrow morning telling me you are better. Mr Perkins promised to deliver a very dirty scrawl in pencil to you which I hope you received.

You cannot imagine how wild I felt when I found you were not at Milk Street on our return from the West. I made sure you would have run up when you found we did not call. Poor dear, I suppose you felt so poorly, and not equal to climbing the great hill of Ludgate. I hope you will spend a nice quiet day at Pinner on Sunday. I can only say I wish I could be with you, don't you think that would be nice. I answer for myself, as and for you, my dear, I am sure you would enjoy it as much as I should.

Before finishing this I must give you a little piece of advice that is for the next three weeks to take things quietly, and not fume and fret yourself about trifles. You will find it much better for yourself and for me also. Now Goodbye, my darling, you have my sincerest wish for recovery, and

Believe me, dearest Sam,

Yours lovingly,

ISABELLA MAYSON

EPSOM,

June 22nd, 1856

MY OWN DARLING SAM,

You cannot imagine how grateful I felt this morning when I received your note telling me you were so much better, and although some parts of the letter were a little bit unkind and cool, that small sentence quite made up for everything sharp although I have no doubt you did not mean it to be so. You have written me so very many loving letters lately that if I receive only one or two pages and those pages very matter of fact, I imagine you are cross with me and don't care so much about me.

Now you are better I am going to ask you a question about the rest of the furniture. I did not like to worry you on Wednesday evening as you seemed so poorly. When shall I come up to finish, because as you well know there are several things to do yet? You can write and let me know what time will suit you best.

I am sorry to tell you Mr and Mrs Kersey have refused

our invitations on account of poor Mr Kersey's health. He does not feel himself sufficiently strong to go out anywhere. I regret it much but I suppose we must put up with the disappointment. All our friends invited have accepted; our numbers bid fair to be very strong. Of course, during Church time this morning, instead of listening to the sound of the Gospel and profiting thereby, I have been giving my imagination full play. I have been thinking how nice it will be at Pinner with the only being I at this moment care for on earth; how kind you will be to poor little me, and how you will say sometimes, "I don't think I shall go to town this morning but stay and have a nice day in the country." You will arrange matters so, won't you, my dear?

I am very, very sorry you are not here to-day. I seem quite lost without you now. Don't you think I shall have a deal to answer for, I mean thinking so much about you, always saying to myself, I wonder what Sam is doing and what he is thinking about, &c. &c. &c. &c.

The time is fast approaching, my precious pet, for our affair. God grant that nothing may happen now to prevent our union, may he give you health and strength to enjoy many many years of happiness with my heart's best love.

Believe me, darling Sam,

Yours with all love's devotion,

BELLA MAYSON

III

Samuel Beeton and Isabella Mayson were married on July 10, 1856, in Epsom Parish Church, the ceremony being performed by the vicar, the Rev. B. Bradney Brocket. The bride looked radiantly beautiful in her white silk wedding-dress flounced to the waist. Each flounce was of a different design, and had been embroidered by one of her sisters. Her bonnet, like those of the bridesmaids, had little flowers resting on her hair in front. There were eight bridesmaids. Three wore pale green and three mauve silk, all with three-tiered skirts. The remaining two, who were children, led the bridesmaid's procession, dressed in white embroidered muslin, hats, and beige boots. They were the bridegroom's half-sister Jessie and the bride's half-sister Lucy.[1]

"It was a gorgeous day, just after the summer meeting," said Lucy, recalling the incident many years later, "and the wedding breakfast was given in the saloon at the Grand Stand. I can still remember how picturesque the guests looked out on the course in front—the big skirts and fringed parasols." The wedding presents, which were displayed in the saloon, included a white piano from Henry Dorling and a toast-rack from his octogenarian father, William, who was still alive at that date. "Though trifling in value," old William Dorling had written to Isabella in the note which accompanied this gift, "I can venture to say there is not one of your numerous friends can be more sincere in wishing you and Mr Beeton all the happiness and prosperity this world can afford."

When the wedding cake had been cut and the usual complimentary toasts drunk in champagne, "a wine of extremely good quality" provided by the bride's stepfather, Henry Dorling, the bridal pair drove off in a

[1] Lucy Dorling, who later married W. H. Smiles, son of Samuel Smiles, author of *Self-Help*, lived to a ripe old age. I met her at her home in Belfast in 1937, when she was in her ninetieth year, and on that occasion she described for my benefit the scene at Epsom as she remembered it eighty years before. She died in Belfast on November 15, 1939, having had eleven children, of whom one was Sir Walter Smiles, M.P.

carriage and pair to Reigate, a distance of nine miles, where they caught the boat train to Folkestone. And so on to Paris.

The honeymoon was spent in France, Germany, and Belgium. The itinerary followed was chosen largely on the recommendation of one of the bridegroom's friends, Frederick Weaklin, who supplied the happy pair with a collection of Murray's guide-books, which proved, in Sam Beeton's words "of immense service, and the greatest comfort to us during our trip into the beautiful south of France." From Paris they travelled to Bordeaux ("the finest commercial city I have seen"), thence to Bassin d'Arcachon, Bayonne, Biarritz ("so pretty, a little haven, so comfortable"), and an excursion into the Pyrenees.

Returning by way of Orleans to Paris, they met Sam's stepmother, and the party went on to Heidelberg to visit Isabella's old school. Finally they managed to see something of Belgium, and reached Dover early in August. It was a memorable honeymoon, for both Sam and Isabella were divinely happy. "My wife," wrote the bridegroom in a letter to his friend Weaklin, "I hardly am used to this word as yet."

IV

By the autumn the household at Pinner was comfortably established. The house was small, but adequately staffed by the standards of the time. A parlour-maid, cook, and gardener were kept, for Isabella was much concerned to conceal the house's somewhat ugly red-brick exterior by creepers and rhododendrons. Sam still worked as hard as ever, and usually caught the last train down from town.

On one occasion, at least, he missed it and had to walk the whole way home, over twelve miles. But, no matter how late he might be, there was always a hot supper waiting for him on his arrival. "I can still remember," wrote Lucy in her old age, "how good it smelt."

Mrs Beeton was never idle, for, besides superintending the needs of her efficiently run household, she took a deep interest in her husband's work. She translated numbers of French stories for his various publications, and contributed weekly notes on dress fashions and cookery to *The English-woman's Domestic Magazine*. The cookery notes formed the basis for the great work which she began to write at this time. Many of them were based on recipes which this magazine's readers were invited by the editor to send in. The request met with an overwhelming response. "To those readers who have favoured us with the results of their experience in cookery, pickling, preserving, etc.," wrote her husband, "we have to tender our best thanks."

"Different people gave their recipes for the book," her sister Lucy recalled.

> That for Baroness Pudding (a suet pudding with a plethora of raisins) was given by the Baroness de Tessier who lived in Epsom. No recipe went into the book without a successful trial, and No. 2 Chandos Villas was the scene of many experiments and some failures. I remember Isabella coming out of the kitchen one day. "This won't do at all," she said and gave me the cake that had turned out like a biscuit. I thought it very good. It had currants in it.

A kind friend, Mrs English, with whom Isabella and her husband used to stay at Newmarket, took a close interest in the project, although she was at first inclined to doubt the authoress's capabilities for the work. "I see difficulties in

F

your way as regards publishing a book on cookery," she wrote to her. "Cookery is a science that is only learnt by long experience and years of study which of course you have not had." However, Mrs English was quite ready to help, and accordingly she introduced Isabella to the Duke of Rutland's cook, Mr Orpwood, who appears to have been very skilled. "I have no doubt he will give you the best advice and assistance," Mrs English told her. "He is a very clever little fellow in his profession and a great economist, and very minute and cleanly in his kitchen." Lord Wilton's cook was another from whom some useful recipes were obtained. "You cannot succeed in compiling a book on cookery," went on Mrs English, "except with the assistance of such persons; for, as I before observed, cookery is a science to be learnt only by long experience and under clever masters and mistresses, and as far as economy goes I prefer a woman if she is a first-rate one." The whole culinary science she finally summed up in a single sentence: "You will find the stockpot is the secret of the kitchen. Without it nothing can be done; with it everything can be done."

In May 1857 their first child, Samuel Orchart, was born. At first he seemed to fare better than the mother, for at the beginning of August the faithful Mrs English wrote:

> I am glad to hear the baby is progressing and doing well. But I do not hear so favourable an account of yourself. However I hope you will improve. As you get stronger you must eat well and drink well. I should think porter or stout would give you strength and be very beneficial to you.

Isabella accordingly took the baby down to Mrs English's house in Newmarket for a change of air, but here, alas, tragedy awaited them. Whether it was that the child caught a chill on the journey or suffered some other form of relapse is not known, but he developed a fever and died soon after their arrival.

Many months passed before Isabella was restored to her former health and strength. Meanwhile she threw herself into her husband's literary interests even more warmly than before, writing, translating, and proof-reading, and a further great consolation was that in September 1859 she gave birth to another son. In the same month the *Book of Household Management*, on which she had been working for over three years, began to appear in monthly parts.

v

At this time the great protagonist of international Free Trade, Richard Cobden, was in Paris trying to come to an understanding with the Emperor Napoleon III and his Minister of Commerce on the subject of tariffs. Indeed, Cobden had gone there with the support of Mr Gladstone, the Chancellor of the Exchequer, and the British Cabinet. In January 1860 his main objective was realized in the conclusion of the far-reaching Commercial Treaty which provided for the mutual reduction of a large range of import duties and opened the way for an era of free trade between the two countries.

With his wife's help Sam Beeton determined to take advantage of this new development in Anglo-French relations. Here was an excellent opportunity, he thought, to improve the appearance of *The Englishwoman's Domestic Magazine* by introducing coloured fashion plates from

France. To arrange the details husband and wife paid a short visit to Paris in the spring of 1860.

A fragmentary diary kept by Isabella on this trip throws some light on their movements during a busy week in the French capital when it snowed and blew intermittently. They stayed at the Hôtel de Rivoli, ate enormous breakfasts of beefsteak and eggs, explored the town between interviews with publishers and printers, and dined sharp at 5.30 P.M., as in Victorian England. Mr Fowler, an English bookseller who had a shop near the Palais Royal, was appointed agent for the distribution of the Beeton publications in France, while M. Adolph Goubaud, of 92 Rue Richelieu, undertook to provide coloured fashion plates and patterns of Berlin needlework.

The Second Empire, against a background of magnificent town-planning by Baron Haussmann and bewitching music by Jacques Offenbach, was then at its height in Paris. This is how the visitors, according to the diary, spent Sunday, March 11, 1860, after they had been to church at the Madeleine:

> From the Madeleine walked into the Place de la Concorde, up the Champs Elysées, beyond the Arc de l'Etoile. Very many houses built since we were in Paris in 1856 . . . grass each side laid out with beds of shrubs. Many carriages, walking people going to the Bois de Boulogne. Very dreary, cold and snowing slightly. The place scarcely looks the same as in summer.
>
> Walked a little way beyond the arch, turned back, walked through the Champs Elysées, Place de la Concorde, through the Jardins des Tuileries and home. Had a little bouillon for lunch, sat down and wrote from Sam's dictation the agreement for Monsieur Goubaud.

Dined at 5.30 in the coffee room, Julienne, Fricandeau de Veau, Poulet à la Marengo, Charlotte Russe. Very nice dinner.

Went at 8 O'clock to Mr Fowler's, 66 Rue Rivoli. Drank tea, chatted with him and came away at 11. Sam finished his prospectus and went to bed.

The colouring of the fashion plates was carried out by the girls in M. Goubaud's workrooms. Isabella went to see this operation, and, although she was unenthusiastic about the plates for the Berlin beadwork, she was pleased with those for the dress models, the results of which looked most attractive. She was quick to realize the possibilities which lay behind the idea of the paper pattern, which had already proved popular with readers of *The Englishwoman's Domestic Magazine*. Copies could be easily made in bulk from a master pattern, so that readers who fancied the model shown in the fashion plate could be supplied with the pattern if they wrote to the editor, or, as Isabella was to put it in the journal, "the full sized paper pattern, tacked together and trimmed, may be had by enclosing 42 stamps." This postal service was to prove a great success, and was destined to be taken up by many imitators.

Three months later the pair took another trip. This time it was more of a holiday, though business followed them round, as it has a habit of doing where those concerned are journalists. They chose Killarney, then, as now, a tourists' paradise. There was, indeed, a tremendous vogue for the lakes in the 1860's. Dion Boucicault was putting the finishing touches to his successful play about this neighbourhood, *The Colleen Bawn*, which Isabella's old music master, Sir Julius Benedict, was to convert into the most popular opera of the period, *The Lily of Killarney*.

It was a gay and adventurous fortnight, which began when their packet-boat ran aground off the Hill of Howth while approaching Kingstown Harbour. Isabella's description of the three main hotels at which they stayed is broadly speaking as true to-day as it was then, for they all three continue to flourish—Jury's in Dublin ("very comfortable quarters"), the Railway Hotel in Killarney ("very comfortable accommodation for ladies"), and the Imperial Hotel in Cork ("a well-managed house"). As for the habits and manners of the people, well, they have not changed much either! "Being market day, most of the people were a little merry," Isabella noted on reaching Killarney; "all of them had had more or less whiskey."

We need not follow them across the lake and up the mountain to the Gap of Dunloe and the other sights which so many thousands have seen before and since. "I always return to Killarney as in some respects the most perfectly beautiful place I have ever known," wrote the historian W. E. H. Lecky, who paid his first visit in 1859.

The lakes, and especially the mountains, are very small as compared with those of Switzerland but the richness and variety of the foliage—arbutus and holly spangling the darker greens—and the beauty of the innumerable islands I have never seen approached, and there is a soft dreamy mist quivering over the mountains and mellowing the landscape which is to my mind the very ideal of poetic beauty.

Like the historian too, the visitors could not fail to have been struck with the people, "the most affectionate, imaginative and quickwitted race."

When it rained, as it did on several days during the trip, Sam and Isabella remained indoors, working on the next number of *The Englishwoman's Domestic Magazine*; in Isabella's words, "Sam with his conversazione and I with the fashions, etc." Thus, while the rain beat down on the windows of Killarney's Railway Hotel, the fashion editress described a riding costume of "nankeen quilting trimmed with white cotton braid and buttons—the short skirt is cut away square on each hip, and forms a tail behind, with pointed facings"—and the editor gave some useful advice to "Young Man," who wished to propose, but was too shy to do so in person. "In affairs of love," wrote Sam to this correspondent in the conversazione column,

> a letter is, out of all question, the most eligible mode of communication. It spares the blushes of the lady, and saves the tyro of a lover a vast deal of *mauvaise honte*. Besides the ladies prefer that a proposal should reach them in black and white, as they have then an opportunity of exhibiting the proof positive of their charms to all their female acquaintances.

They were in Killarney on July 10, "the anniversary of our wedding day," Isabella noted in her diary. "Have been married four years ago today. How the time slips away."

There was indeed little time left for Isabella Beeton, but enough to complete the work by which she is best known. In October 1861 the *Book of Household Management*, popularly known as "Mrs Beeton's Cookery Book," made its appearance from her husband's publishing offices in the Strand.

Chapter IV

HOUSEHOLD MANAGEMENT

THE success of Mrs Beeton's *Book of Household Management* was foreshadowed by a significant incident which occurred about twenty years before its publication. A woman writer named Eliza Acton—not Mrs Beeton, as has sometimes been stated—called on the publishing house of Longman, and offered its head some verse of her own composition. "My dear Madam," said Thomas Longman, "it is no good bringing me poetry; nobody wants poetry now. Bring me a cookery book, and we might come to terms." The publisher spoke more in jest than in earnest, but Eliza Acton took him at his word. She set to work and produced a volume which Longman duly published under the title of *Modern Cookery*. The work had an immediate and rapid sale, and shortly afterwards, to please the authoress, Longman published her poems. This venture attracted not the slightest interest on the part of the public. The cookery book, however, continued to be in demand for many years.

Mrs Beeton's book was wider in scope than Eliza Acton's, and, it seems scarcely necessary to add, the reward it reaped was more than proportionately greater. It embraced the whole field of domestic science. In the words of its sub-title, it was a work

comprising information for the mistress, housekeeper, cook, kitchen-maid, butler, footman, coachman, valet, upper and under house-maids, lady's maid, maid-of-all-work, laundry maid, nurse and nurse-maid, monthly, wet, and sick nurses, etc., etc., also sanitary, medical and legal memoranda; with a history of the origin, properties, and uses, of all things connected with home life and comfort.

It originally appeared in twenty-four monthly parts, price 3d. each, which ran from November 1859 to October 1861. In the latter year it was reissued in book form, consisting of over half a million words and comprising in all 1172 pages of small and closely spaced print, 500 wood engravings, and 50 coloured plates. She was particularly pleased with these plates, which she proudly described as "a novelty not without value." The price of this amazing production was 7s. 6d. In 1863 the recipes which it contained, and the other parts relating to the kitchen, with a number of alterations and additions, were published separately as *The Englishwoman's Cookery Book*.

The motives which impelled Mrs Beeton to undertake the work are stated in the preface to the first edition of *Household Management*—namely, "the discomfort and suffering which I had seen brought upon men and woman by household mismanagement." What more worthy motives could she have had? "I have always thought," Mrs Beeton goes on,

that there is no more fruitful source of family discontent than a housewife's badly cooked dinners and untidy ways. Men are now so well served out of doors—at their clubs, well-ordered taverns and dining-houses—that, in order to compete with the attractions of these places, a mistress must be thoroughly acquainted with the theory and practice of cookery, as well as be perfectly conversant with all the other arts of making and keeping a comfortable home.

As might be expected, the chapters devoted to cookery form the greater part of the book, and Mrs Beeton is at some pains to explain how they are set out. "In this book," she says,

> I have attempted to give, under the chapters devoted to cookery, an intelligible arrangement to every recipe, a list of the *ingredients*, a plain statement of the *mode* of preparing each dish, and a careful estimate of its *cost*, the *number of people* for whom it is *sufficient*, and the time when it is *seasonable*. . . . But in the department belonging to the Cook I have striven, too, to make my book something more than a Cookery Book, and have, therefore, on the best authority I could obtain, given an account of the natural history of the animals and vegetables which we use as food. I have followed the animal from his birth to his appearance on the table; have described the manner of feeding him and of slaying him, the position of his various joints, and after giving the recipes, have described the modes of carving Meat, Poultry and Game.

II

We may now approach the model Victorian household from Mrs Beeton's own particular point of view, taking as our text the first edition of the *Household Management*.

First to be considered is the all-important being on whom every household depends for its good order and management—the mistress. "As with the commander of an army or the leader of any enterprise," writes Mrs Beeton,

> so it is with the mistress of the house. Her spirit will be seen through the whole establishment; and just in proportion as she performs her duties intelligently and thoroughly, so

will her domestics follow in her path. Of all these acquirements, which more particularly belong to the feminine character, there are none which takes a higher rank in our estimation than such as enter into a knowledge of household duties; for on these are perpetually dependent the happiness, comfort, and well being of a family.

The authoress thereupon proceeds to describe some of the domestic virtues which are necessary in a mistress to the proper management of a household. These include cleanliness, frugality, discriminating friendships, hospitality, good temper, and above all *early rising*. The latter is

not only the parent of health but of innumerable other advantages. Indeed when a mistress is an early riser, it is almost certain that her house will be orderly and well-managed. On the contrary, if she remains in bed till a late hour, then the domestics, who, as we have before observed, invariably partake somewhat of their mistress's character, will surely become sluggards.

In these circumstances it is not uninstructive to follow the ideal mistress in an average day in her life:

Having risen early, as we have already advised, and having given due attention to the bath and made a careful toilet, it will be well at once to see that the children have received their proper ablutions and are in every way clean and comfortable. The first meal of the day, breakfast, will then be served, at which all the family should be punctually present, unless illness or other circumstances prevent. After breakfast is over, it will be well for the mistress of the house to make a round of the kitchen and other offices to see that all are in order and that the morning's work has been properly performed by the various domestics. The orders of the day should then be given and questions which the domestics desire to ask respecting their several departments should be answered, and any special articles they may require handed to them from the store-closet. After this general super-intendence of her servants, the mistress, if the mother of a young family, may devote herself to the instruction of some of its younger members or to the examination of the state of their wardrobes, leaving the later portion of the morning for reading or for some amusing recreation.

Having thus got through the morning, or, as Mrs Beeton puts it, "these duties and pleasures being per-formed and enjoyed," the mistress now partakes of luncheon. "It should be a light meal," we are told, "but its solidity must of course in some degree be proportionate to the time it is intended to enable you to wait for your dinner and the amount of exercise you take in the mean-time." Special provision is made for the children, who are assumed to be a necessary part of the household, and who must have their principal meal served in the middle of the day.

In many houses where a nursery dinner is provided for the children about one o'clock the mistress and the elder portion of the family make their luncheon at the same time from the same joint, or whatever may be provided. A mistress will arrange according to circumstances the serving of the meal; but the more usual plan is for the lady of the house to have the joint brought to her table and afterwards carried to the nursery.

After luncheon is over comes the time for the mistress to pay and receive "morning calls." The more formal of these should not exceed twenty minutes in duration, and the lady paying the visit "may remove her boa or necker-chief, but neither her shawl nor bonnet." They are paid in various circumstances, but are always required "after dining at a friend's house, or after a ball, picnic, or any other party." The model visitor should choose a suitable time for calling and in the case of "visits of friendship" avoid staying too long, for "the courtesies of society should ever be maintained, even in the domestic circle and among the nearest friends."

During these visits the manners should be easy and cheerful and the subjects of conversation such as may be readily terminated. Serious discussions or arguments are to be altogether avoided, and there is much danger and impropriety in expressing opinions of those persons and characters with whom perhaps there is but a slight acquaintance. . . . If the mistress be a wife, never let an account of her husband's failings pass her lips.

There are two other subjects, besides a husband's failings, which should not be introduced at morning calls. These are the caller's dogs and her children:

It is not advisable at any time to take favourite dogs into another lady's drawing-room, for many persons have an absolute dislike to such animals: and besides this there is always a chance of a breakage of some article occurring through their leaping and bounding here and there, sometimes very much to the fear and annoyance of the hostess. Her children, also, unless they are particularly well trained and orderly and she is on exceedingly friendly terms with the hostess, should not accompany a lady in making morning calls. Where a lady, however, pays her visits in a carriage, the children can be taken in the vehicle and remain in it until the visit is over.

The morning calls being over and "their etiquette properly attended to," there comes the next great event of the day which claims the mistress's attention—namely, dinner. For this meal, especially when there is "company," careful preparations must be made. The invited guests must be selected so that they will be suited to each other, and much of the pleasure of a dinner-party will depend upon their arrangement at table "so as to form a due admixture to talkers and listeners, the grave and the gay." We now reach what is the most trying time for the hostess:

The half hour before dinner has always been considered as the great ordeal through which the mistress in giving a dinner party will either pass with flying colours or lose many of her laurels. The anxiety to receive her guests—her hope that all will be present in due time—her trust in the skill of her cook and the attention of the other domestics— all tend to make these few minutes a trying time. The mistress, however, must display no kind of agitation but show her tact in suggesting light and cheerful subjects of conversation, which will be much aided by the introduction of any particular new book, curiosity of art, or article of vertu, which may pleasantly engage the attention of the company. Photograph albums, crest albums, new music, will aid to pass a few moments pleasantly.

"In giving an entertainment of this kind," Mrs Beeton wisely adds,

the mistress should remember that it is her duty to make her guests feel happy, comfortable, and quite at their ease; and the guests should also consider that they have come to the house of their hostess to be happy. Thus an opportunity is given to all for innocent enjoyment and intellectual improvement. When also acquaintances may be formed that may prove invaluable through life and information gained that will enlarge the mind. Many celebrated men and women have been great talkers; and amongst others the genial

Sir Walter Scott, who spoke freely to everyone, and a favourite remark of whom it was that he never did so without learning something he didn't know before.

When the guests are seated at the dinner-table they should observe certain well-established rules. One of these is "not to ask for soup or fish twice, as in doing so part of the company may be kept waiting too long for the second course, when perhaps a little revenge is taken by looking at the awkward consumer of a second portion." Again, when the finger-glasses which accompany the dessert are placed on the table it will be sufficient for the ladies present to wet the tips of their fingers. "The French and other continentals have a habit of gargling the mouth; but it is a custom which no English gentlewoman should in the slightest degree imitate."

Here Mrs Beeton refers to the practice of "taking wine" with individual guests, which she remarks has now been abolished at many tables. However, where it is still kept up it should not begin until the fish or soup is finished, when the gentleman honoured by sitting on the hostess's right may politely inquire if she will do him the honour of taking wine with him. "This will act as a signal to the rest of the company, the gentleman of the house most probably requesting the same pleasure of the ladies at his right and left."

Mrs Beeton's remarks on the withdrawing of the ladies at the conclusion of dinner are peculiarly piquant, and are of especial interest since they include one of the comparatively few references to the appearance of the male of the species in the mistress's well-ordered *curriculum vitæ*.

In the first place she is inclined to agree with Dr Johnson's opinion of "the effects of dinner on men":

Before dinner men meet with great inequality of understanding; and those who are conscious of this inferiority
have the modesty not to talk. When they have drunk wine,
every man feels himself happy and loses that modesty, and
grows impudent and vociferous; but he is not improved, he
is only not sensible of his defects.

This judgment is rather severe, says Mrs Beeton, "but
there may be some truth in it."

"When the fruit has been taken and a glass or two of
wine passed round," she continues,

the time will have arrived when the hostess will rise, and
thus give the signal for the ladies to leave the gentlemen
and retire to the drawing room. The gentlemen of the
party will rise at the same time, and he who is nearest the
door will open it for the ladies, all remaining courteously
standing until the last lady has withdrawn. . . . In former
times when the bottle circulated freely among the guests,
it was necessary for the ladies to retire earlier than they do
at present, for the gentlemen of the company soon became
unfit to conduct themselves with that decorum which is
essential in the presence of ladies. Thanks however to the
improvements in modern society and the high example
shown to the nation by its most illustrious personages, tem-
perance is in these happy days a striking feature in the
character of a gentleman. Delicacy of conduct towards the
female sex has increased with the esteem in which they are
now universally held, and thus the very early withdrawing
of the ladies from the dining room is to be deprecated.

Mrs Beeton also deprecates the custom of "non-intro-
duction" at evening parties and balls in private houses,
where the guests are left to discover for themselves the
position and qualities of the people around them.

The servant, indeed, calls out the names of all the visitors as they arrive, but, in many instances, mispronouncing them; so that it will not be well to follow this information as if it were an unerring guide. In our opinion, it is a cheerless and depressing custom, although in thus speaking, we do not allude to the large assemblies of the aristocracy, but to the smaller parties of the middle classes.

At balls in private houses a lady should not refuse the invitation of a gentleman to dance unless she is previously engaged.

The hostess must be supposed to have asked to the house only those persons whom she knows to be perfectly respectable and of unblemished character, as well as pretty equal in position, and thus, to decline the offer of any gentleman present, would be a tacit reflection on the master and mistress of the house.

For the especial benefit of the young who will read the book Mrs Beeton is careful to add that

introductions at balls and evening parties cease with the occasion that calls them forth, no introduction, at these times, giving a gentleman a right to address, afterwards, a lady. She is, consequently, free next morning to pass her partner at a ball of the previous evening without the slightest recognition.

We may conclude this short survey of the mistress's day with Mrs Beeton's account of the family dinner and "the manner of passing evenings at home." As regards the family dinner at home which

compared with either giving or going to a dinner party is of course of much more frequent occurrence, and many will say, of much greater importance . . . here we will only say

G

that for both mistress and servants, as well in large as small households, it will be found by far the better plan to cook and serve the dinner and to lay the table cloth and the sideboard with the same cleanliness, neatness, and scrupulous exactness, whether it be for the mistress herself alone, a small family, or for "company." If this rule be strictly adhered to, all will find themselves increase in managing skill; whilst a knowledge of their daily duties will become familiar and enable them to meet difficult occasions with ease and overcome any amount of obstacles.

"Of the manner of passing evenings at home," Mrs Beeton continues,

there is none pleasanter than in such recreative enjoyments as those which relax the mind from its severer duties, whilst they stimulate it with a gentle delight. Where there are young people forming part of the evening circle, interesting and agreeable pastime should especially be promoted. It is of incalculable benefit to them that their homes should possess all the attractions of healthful amusement, comfort and happiness; for if they do not find pleasure there they will seek it elsewhere. It ought, therefore, to enter into the domestic policy of every parent to make her children feel that home is the happiest place in the world; that to imbue them with this precious home-feeling is one of the choicest gifts a parent can bestow. Light or fancy needlework often forms a portion of the evening's recreation for the ladies of the household, and this may be varied by an occasional game at chess and backgammon. It has often been remarked too that nothing is more delightful to the feminine members of a family than the reading aloud of some good standard work or amusing publication. A knowledge of polite literature may be thus obtained by the whole family, especially if the reader is able and willing to explain the more difficult passages of the book and expatiate on the wisdom and beauties it may contain. . . . Musical evenings make additional attractions for home and increase its pleasures. Where music is cultivated by the mistress of a house or by the daughters, husbands and brothers are generally found "at home" in the evenings.

We need not follow the mistress further in her campaign. In such matters as choosing a house, engaging servants, and giving a letter of introduction to a friend she must be guided by the same high-minded principles as elsewhere in the household. Her position in the social life of the nation is by no means a negligible one. "She ought always to remember," says Mrs Beeton in summing up her character and giving her final advice,

> that she is the first and last, the Alpha and the Omega in the government of her establishment; and that it is by her conduct that its whole internal policy is regulated. She is therefore a person of far more importance in a community than she usually thinks she is. On her pattern her daughters model themselves; by her counsels they are directed; through her virtues all are honoured:—"her children rise up and call her blessed; her husband also; and he praiseth her."
>
> Therefore, let each mistress always remember her responsible position, never approving a mean action or speaking an unrefined word. Let her conduct be such that her inferiors may respect her, and such as an honourable and right-minded man may look for in his wife and the mother of his children. Let her think of the many compliments and the sincere homage that have been paid to her sex by the greatest philosophers and writers, both in ancient and modern times. . . . Cherishing then in her breast the respected utterances of the good and the great, let the

mistress of every house rise to the responsibility of its management; so that in doing her duty to all around her she may receive the genuine reward of respect, love and affection.

III

Cookery is rightly regarded by Mrs Beeton as an art. In the early stages of human development "only to live" was the great object of mankind; but with multiplication of comforts and accumulation of riches new wants were created. "The object then," remarks Mrs Beeton,

> is not only to *live* but to live economically, agreeably, tastefully and well. Accordingly the art of cookery commences; and although the fruits of the earth, the fowls of the air, the beasts of the field, and the fish of the sea are still the only food of mankind, yet these are so prepared, improved, and dressed by skill and ingenuity, that they are the means of immeasureably extending the human enjoyments. Everything that is edible and passes under the hands of the cook is more or less changed and assumes new forms. Hence the influence of that functionary is immense upon the happiness of a household.

As for the kitchen itself, it is "the great laboratory of every household," and much of the "weal or woe" of bodily health depends upon the nature of the preparations concocted within its walls.

The duties of the cook and the kitchen- and scullery-maids are described with the same thoroughness and conscientiousness as those of the mistress.

As a preliminary to kitchen duties, she described in felicitous language how the cooks of the Middle Ages gave their orders from a high chair which commanded a view of "all that was going on in their several domains." The cook held a long wooden spoon,

> with which he tasted without leaving his seat, the various comestibles that were cooking on the stoves, and which he frequently used as a rod of punishment on the backs of those whose idleness and gluttony too largely predominated over their diligence and temperance.

Lest her readers should imagine that the office of the scullery-maid is unduly menial and degrading, Mrs Beeton has some comforting observations to make on it, and, incidentally, in praise of Victorian diligence and industry. "The position of scullery-maid is not, of course, one of high rank," she says,

> nor is the payment for her services large. But if she be fortunate to have ever had a good kitchen-maid and a clever cook, she may very soon learn to perform various little duties connected with cooking operations, which may be of considerable service in fitting her for a more responsible place. Now, it will be doubtless thought by the majority of our readers that the fascinations connected with the position of scullery-maid are not so great as to induce many people to leave a comfortable home in order to work in a scullery. But we are acquainted with one instance in which the desire on the part of a young girl was so strong to become connected with the kitchen and cookery that she absolutely left her parents and engaged herself as a scullery-maid in a gentleman's house. Here she showed herself so active and intelligent that she very quickly rose to the rank of kitchen-maid; and from this, so great was her gastronomical genius, she became in a short space of time one of the best woman cooks in England.

The greater part of the book is, of course, devoted to the preparation and serving of food. Something has already been said of the manner in which Mrs Beeton obtained many of her recipes. Friends and correspondents in France and Germany, besides England, Scotland, and Ireland, readily placed their ideas at her disposal. "A diligent study of the works of the best writers on modern cookery," she tells us, "was also necessary to the faithful fulfilment of my task." The headmistress of her old school in Heidelberg, for instance, presented her with a very useful collection of German recipes. Many of the interesting historical notes and anecdotes, omitted from later editions, owe their inspiration to *Beeton's Dictionary of Universal Information*, which her husband compiled about the same time. The story of "Baroness Pudding" has been told, and many people have endorsed Mrs Beeton's opinion when she says that this pudding "cannot be too highly recommended; . . . with all who have partaken of it, it is an especial favourite."

Here is the description of the origin of the well-known *Poulet à la Marengo* which she got from her husband. The dish was first served after the engagement at Marengo, in North-western Italy, in which Napoleon Bonaparte, then First Consul of France, defeated the Austrians on June 14, 1800.

On the evening of the battle the First Consul was very hungry after the agitation of the day, and a fowl was ordered with all expedition. The fowl was procured, but there was no butter at hand, and unluckily none could be found in the neighbourhood. There was oil in abundance, however, and the cook having poured a certain quantity into his skillet, put in the fowl with a clove of garlic and other seasoning, with a little white wine, the best the country afforded. He then garnished it with mushrooms and served it up hot. The dish proved the second conquest of the day, as the First Consul found it most agreeable to his palate and expressed his satisfaction. Ever since a fowl à la Marengo is a favourite dish with all lovers of good cheer.

Mrs Beeton has earned a reputation for extravagance. Nothing could be further from the truth; for, as we have seen, her great object in writing the *Household Management* was to meet the demand for an economical cookery book, and all the original recipes were carefully studied with that object in view before they were included in the book. Many of these were discarded as being too economical in later editions, particularly during the Edwardian period, when the work was edited by a German-Swiss, Herr Hermann Senn, and unfortunately lost the authoress's characteristic touch which made it such an English classic. Most of Mrs Beeton's soup recipes, for example, were for those cheap soups used in France and Germany—cabbage soup, bread soup, soup made from pea-pods, etc. The secret of *Soup à la Solferino*, which falls within this category, and still appears on menus, was communicated to Mrs Beeton by an English newspaper correspondent who was present at the battle of Solferino in 1859, during the struggle for Italian independence, and who was invited by some of Victor Emmanuel's troops, on the day before the battle, to partake of a portion of their *potage*. "He willingly enough consented, and found that these clever campaigners had made a most palatable dish from very easily procured materials."[1]

---

[1] Benjamin Vulliamy. He later became a close friend and neighbour of the Beetons, and stood godfather to their youngest son, Mayson.

Soup à la cantatrice, whose principal ingredients were sago and eggs, was described by Isabella as "an excellent soup very beneficial for the voice." It owed its inclusion to Jenny Lind, "the celebrated Swedish nightingale," as Isabella called her: she habitually consumed it "with considerable advantage to the voice in singing."

Another interesting soup owes its origin to the fact that it was first used by Mrs Beeton herself for distribution among the poor families of Pinner in 1858. "It was a hard winter that year," writes her sister Mrs Smiles, "and the poor children of the neighbourhood came regularly with their cans for soup. Each week they brought bigger cans." The principal ingredients were ox-head, meat-bones, celery, leeks, turnips, and, surprisingly enough, beer. It appears in the *Household Management* under the appropriate title of "Useful Soups for Benevolent Purposes." The cost was not great, and, as Mrs Beeton said, she had reason to believe

> that the soup was very much liked and gave to the members of those families a dish of warm, comforting food in place of the cold meat and piece of bread which form with too many cottagers their usual meal, when with a little more knowledge of the "cooking" art they might have for less expense a warm dish every day.

Throughout the work, indeed, Mrs Beeton had always an eye for economy. "Rice," we learn, "with proper management in cooking it, forms a very valuable and cheap addition to our farinaceous food, and in years of scarcity has been found eminently useful in lessening the consumption of flour." Baked rice pudding is, therefore, described as "plain and economical, a nice Pudding for Children." It works out at an average cost of from 2*d*.

to 7*d*. per head according to the ingredients used. So also in the case of suet pudding served with roast meat. "Most children like this accompaniment to roast meat," says Mrs Beeton.

> Where there is a large family of children and the means of keeping them are limited, it is a most economical plan to serve up the pudding before the meat; as in this case the consumption of the latter article will be much smaller than it otherwise would be.

Mrs Beeton wrote for households where eight or ten children were not uncommon, and the quantities of ingredients employed in her recipes had to provide for more mouths than the average household to-day. In her cake-making, which most frequently forms the basis of the charge of extravagance, this consideration should be borne in mind, but even here she never began with "take a dozen eggs," which has become a music-hall joke. She was, however, responsible for several well-proved maxims of domestic economy, such as "A place for everything and everything in its place," and "Clean as you go, for muddle makes more muddle."

If Isabella Beeton always had an eye for economy, it was never at the expense of civilized living. "Dine we must," she said, "and we may as well dine elegantly as well as wholesomely."

IV

In the passages dealing with "the origin, properties and uses of all things connected with home life and comfort," Mrs Beeton is most stimulating. Helped by her husband, she brings a sound knowledge of the humanities to her assistance. She quotes Homer and Pliny, for instance, on the subject of parsley, and refers to Linnæus when discussing the size of the dace. The gastronomic habits of the ancient Romans come in for frequent comment, such, for example, as their love of fish. "Apicius offered a prize to anyone who could invent a new brine compounded of the liver of red mullets," she relates;

> and Lucullus had a canal cut through a mountain in the neighbourhood of Naples that fish might be the more easily transported to the gardens of his villa. Hortensius, the orator, wept over the death of a turbot which he had fed with his own hands; and the daughter of Druses adorned one that she had with rings of gold. These were surely instances of misplaced affection; but there is no accounting for tastes.

Mrs Beeton's fish recipes are perhaps the least satisfactory part of the book, but she did not regard fish as a main dish, except for invalids, and it should be remembered that the extent to which fish has become a popular article of diet has greatly increased through the uses of road transport and refrigeration.

Some of her remarks too on the animals which form the subjects of the culinary art are worthy of quotation. Take her description of the "Tony pig," or *Anthony*, "so named, it is presumed, from being the one always assigned to the Church, when tithe was taken in kind, and as St Anthony was the patron of husbandry, his name was given in a sort of bitter derision to the starveling that constituted his dues." This description is taken from her "Several Observations on the Common Hog."

"However few or however many young pigs there may be in the farrow," she writes in this chapter,

there is always one who is the dwarf of the family circle, a poor shrivelled half starved anatomy, with a small melancholy voice, a staggering gait, a woe-begone countenance and a thread of a tail, whose existence the complacent mother ignores, his plethoric brothers and sisters repudiate, and for whose emaciated jaws there is never a spare or supplemental teat, till one of the favoured gormandizers overtaken by a momentary oblivion drops the lacteal fountain and gives the little squeaking struggler the chance of a momentary mouthful.

Contrast this miserable object of pity with the well-nourished Chinese pig, which Mrs Beeton notices with enthusiastic approval:

He has a broad snout, short head, eyes bright and fiery, very small fine pink ears, wide cheeks, high chine, with a neck of such immense thickness, that when the animal is fat it looks like an elongated carcase—a mass of fat without shape or form, like a feather pillow. The belly is dependent and almost trailing on the ground, the legs very short, and the tail so small as to be little more than a rudiment. It has a ravenous appetite, and will eat anything that the wonderful assimilating powers of its stomach can digest; and to that capability there seems no limit in the range of animal or vegetable nature. The consequence of this perfect and singularly rapid digestion is an unprecedented proneness to obesity, a process of fattening that once commenced goes on with such rapid development that in a short time it loses all form, depositing such an amount of fat that it in fact ceases to have any refuse part of offal beyond the hair on its back and the callous extremity of the snout *the whole carcase is eatable*.

Here and there also one meets with a flash of humour, though it may be unconscious. Writing of sheep, for instance, she says:

The great object of the grazier is to procure an animal which will yield the greatest pecuniary return in the shortest time. All sheep will not do this alike; some, *like men*, are so restless and irritable that no system of feeding however good will develop their frames or make them fat.

In this, perhaps, lies Mrs Beeton's philosophy of cookery. Leanness in both man and beast was, in Mrs Beeton's opinion, synonymous with irritability. Both must be fattened to make them complacent, and Mrs Beeton can brook nothing but unconditional surrender.

Again, in the chapter devoted to "The Doctor," Mrs Beeton makes a grim jest in outlining instructions "How to Bleed." "When a person is bled," she says,

he should always be standing, or at any rate in the sitting position: for if, as is often the case, he should happen to faint he can, in most cases at least, easily be brought to again by the operator placing him flat on his back and stopping the bleeding. *This is of the greatest importance.* It has been recommended, for what supposed advantages we don't know, to bleed people when they are lying down. Should a person under these circumstances faint what can be done to bring him to again? The great treatment of lowering the body of the patient to the flat position cannot be followed here. It is in that position already, and cannot be placed lower than it at present is—except, as is most likely to be the case, under the ground.

Taken all in all, however, the *Household Management* filled a great gap in the lives of the later Victorians, and rendered yeoman service to hearth and home. Well might the young housewife turn to it for a solution to all her difficulties. If she wished to know how to cure apoplexy or engage a butler, to cook truffles or explain the laundry-maid's duties, treat scarlet fever or take a house on lease, she could not do better than consult Mrs Beeton. The hero in Conan Doyle's amusing novel of married life, *A Duet with an Occasional Chorus*, states it as his opinion that "*this book contains more wisdom to the square inch than any work of man.*" This is an eloquent testimonial, but also a true one, for the edition in question contained more than 80,000 square inches of closely packed information.

V

From the day of publication *Mrs Beeton's Book of Household Management* was in constant demand. In the first year over 60,000 copies were sold, and a second edition was called for. This appeared in 1863. The authoress received many letters containing appreciative criticisms and suggested additions. Among these was one from the noted woman writer Harriet Martineau, who was slowly dying of heart disease. Mrs Beeton had sent her a presentation copy of the work.

AMBLESIDE,
March 4, 1862

DEAR MRS BEETON,

I have never had any idea of taking advantage of your kind thoughtfulness in desiring me not to write, even to acknowledge your book: but I have waited to read it, or as much of it as is meant to be *read*, properly speaking. In my feeble condition, I feel it allowable, in a general way, to acknowledge the arrival of this sort of gift by the hand of my niece before reading them: but your book tempted me to wait, and finally write myself. It has given me a great deal of pleasure; and my niece, who relieves me of house-keeping, and is a first-rate housewife, declares the book to be very valuable indeed in the cookery part. To us it seems new to state the cost of the dishes, and to the last degree useful. In course of time we shall have gone over a great deal of your ground with much thankfulness to you.

The specifications of the duties of Servants are excellent too. The parts we least like are the instructions on Manners, and in Medical matters. Being homeopaths, we think the latter very dangerous—while aware that that part is from a professional hand. I just say this much for honesty's sake, and because I know, from my own experience, that one is glad to hear what people think when a second edition of one's book may afford an opportunity for reconsideration —whether one remains finally of the same opinion or not.

In the nineteen-twentieths of the book I think we may delight and rejoice; and I heartily wish you joy of it.

Believe me truly your obliged,

HARRIET MARTINEAU

Many humbler readers echoed Miss Martineau's good wishes and endorsed her finding that the work was "to the last degree useful." "I consider it an excellent work," was the verdict of "a practical cook of great experience" in returning the book to her mistress. "It is full of useful information about everything, and I should say one might learn to cook from it who never tried before."

Throughout the next half-century it came as the most welcome wedding gift to thousands of young housewives, who were able to build up and maintain happy and com-fortable homes on its foundation. It is not merely the recipes which make the work significant, important as these are in themselves, but Mrs Beeton's attitude to cookery as an art and the great part which she assigns to it in the life of the nation. Read now as she wrote it, the book is a valuable social document, and it must always rank as a leading authority on Victorian ideals and Victorian family life. The substitution for its help in our own day of cookery columns in the daily and weekly papers may tell modern housewives all they want to know, but it has deprived those who depend exclusively upon them of a work which was their mothers' and grandmothers' great standby.

It is satisfactory to know, however, that in its modern dress the book is still in great demand. It has recently been brought up to date by a team of experts in the light of post-war food problems and cooking methods. If not quite so rich in illustrations, the latest edition (1950) has nearly as many pages as the original version and about the same number of recipes. There are chapters on etiquette, the law, the nursery, the "home doctor," and even pressure cookery. The "practical, reliable, and economical Mrs Beeton" has indeed stood the test of time, and her reputation is now firmly established as the authoress of the best-known British cookery-book. It is all the more remarkable, therefore, that her name and achievements should find no place in the British *Dictionary of National Biography*.

Chapter V

GOOD FORTUNE AND BAD FORTUNE

THE Beetons made their home at Pinner for five years. It was a period of supreme happiness for both, and it was clouded only by the death of their two elder children in infancy. The first died in 1857, and the second, also a boy, at the close of 1862.

The second child died suddenly in Brighton from some illness, probably scarlet fever. Among the letters of sympathy which Samuel Beeton received on this occasion was one from his stepmother, who, it will be remembered, had inherited The Dolphin and had later married its manager, Isaac Wyatt. It is the only letter from her which has survived, and it shows evidence of the good relations existing between them, even after her second marriage. Apparently she made all the funeral arrangements in Norwood Cemetery, where the child was buried.

"I shall, if I do not hear from you," she wrote,

> go down to the Junction to meet you and bring dear Bella here. If you will come, do dear Sam come here, at any rate till Monday. It will be too much to go home alone. Come to us. Mr Wyatt feels much for you both, and on Sunday we can be so quiet. . . . I cannot express half I feel for you both, and I can assure you all here feel your loss their own.

In 1863, probably the early summer, Samuel and Isabella Beeton left their home at Pinner and came up to town to

live for a short period "over the shop" in the Strand.
The move was doubtless made because the lease of the
Pinner house had expired, and they thought London the
most convenient place in which to live while looking for
another house. Inside a month or so Samuel Beeton
acquired a converted farmhouse called Mount Pleasant
down the river at Greenhithe, which boasted a greenhouse,
croquet lawn, flagpole, and two acres of land. It was here
that their third child, whom they called Orchart, was born
on New Year's Eve.

This latest addition to the family was a robust baby
with ruddy cheeks, and he thrived from the beginning.
His appearance completed his parents' happiness. Everything seemed to be going well. Business was prospering,
both were working hard, but they both found time for
recreation and more trips to the Continent. Sam acquired
a mare called Gertie, which he used to ride round the
fields and lanes near Greenhithe. In the summer of 1863
they made a trip to Germany, and in the following year
they returned to France. There was probably some faint
pretext of business for these trips, but they were really
holidays, and Sam and Isabella Beeton thoroughly enjoyed
themselves, as they had done in Ireland.

Husband and wife arrived in Berlin on a Sunday afternoon in July, and straight away plunged into an orgy of
sightseeing. We need not follow them round Charlotten-
burg, Sans Souci, Babelsburg, and the other royal palaces,
at all of which they seem to have been cordially received.
The English were most popular in Prussia at this time;
indeed, it was only five years before that Queen Victoria's
eldest daughter, the Princess Royal, had married the
Prussian Crown Prince Frederick. "She is very much

liked in Prussia and seems quite to have won the German hearts," noted Isabella of the last Kaiser's mother in her diary. "Every time she goes out in her carriage, everybody takes off their hats and much more enthusiasm is displayed whenever she is seen in public than any other member of the Prussian Royal Family."

From Berlin they went on to Dresden, the unspoiled baroque capital of the independent kingdom of Saxony. There were more castles, picture-galleries, and visits to the opera, where they saw a performance of *Masaniello*, but thought the singing bad. Crossing the Elbe, they climbed the Basten. "Huge overhanging and perpendicular rocks," noted Isabella. "Good walking, the view of the Elbe and the surrounding country one of the most lovely pictures imaginable."

Next year it was much the same in France, except that they managed to get in some racing, in addition to sightseeing, and a little business. They drove out to Longchamps to see the Grand Prix, for which an English horse, Blair Atholl, who had won the Derby, was favourite. But the Channel crossing seems to have upset Blair Atholl, since he was beaten easily by a comparative outsider. Sam reported the race for *Sporting Life*, a journal in whose production he had lately come to take an interest, and he also took a lot of notes for his other readers. "Mr Dorling and cardmakers might be imported advantageously," he noted jocularly, since he did not think much of the French racecards. On the other hand, he thought the women smarter than at Epsom. "Before your eyes there sit the most elegantly dressed women in the world. Perchance our own women may be approaching the standard of *les modes françaises* under Madame Goubaud's tuition, yet there is a wide, wide difference between the *manière d'être* of a Frenchwoman and an Englishwoman." But Isabella, with her practical eye, attributed the difference, at any rate at Longchamps, to "complete absence of poverty."

A letter from Sam Beeton to his wife belonging to this later period was written from Newmarket, where he was staying with his friends the Englishes in the autumn of 1864, after their return from their holiday in France. It contains a reference to their first child, who had died here in the second year of their marriage. Its chief interest, however, lies in the evidence which it contains of the real literary and working partnership which existed between husband and wife. Not only did Sam rely on his wife for contributions to his magazines in the shape of cookery and dressmaking notes and translations of French stories, but he also consulted her on such technical questions as "lay-out" and "make-up." This letter is concerned with the first number of *The Young Englishwoman*, which went to press at this time.

WARREN VILLA,
NEWMARKET,
Oct. 11, 64

MY DEAREST,

I shall not be home till Friday evening, I think, for I want to see one or two men who will not be here till to-morrow.

Prince Soltikoff has been admiring the mare, and by a little humouring, it's just possible one will land 100 g's for her. I think I had better go into the horse dealing line.

I have asked Sidney to get Young to write *his* notions on paper of what the Young E'woman shd. be, irrespectively of mine, and if Y is there to-morrow, as I think he will be, ask Sidney to let you see him, and you can tell him what *you* think. Of course you will know, as the French say, how to tell him this without expressg. any opinion abt. the wisdom of the step. Because that is *toute autre question*.

Send the description of the 8 pages you have already got up for the Young E'woman as soon as pos' with the clichés to Cox and Wyman and ask C.W. to let Poulter do the making up. These done, the next thing is the Sheet of Dble Demy with 2 sets of diagrams and Needlework patterns, given us, that is to say, the Suppt. for the Y. E'woman for 2 weeks. These two sheets of Dble Demy (the pattern already pasted down and the diagrams as just mentioned) will set us right for 6 weeks. With No. 1 I suppose we had better issue the Patterns and Diagrams 8 pp. that is to say. *N'est-ce-pas?*

Friend E. is very cordial and excessively kind. I have enclosed this in a note to Sidney wh. will get to the Strand this evening 5 o'c. or before, and have asked him to go down or send a telegram to you that I shall not be home.

Give my best kisses to our dear little pet—one slept in the room last night—and it made my heart ache, you may know—where our first little chappy went away from us. Preserve to us our present joy, and we can bear a good deal of trouble, having that.

Goodbye, my girl, "Sweet kisses on thy fair-formed brow I'd give, but can't just now."

Receive, I pray you my good master, the assurance of my highest consideration, the intimation of my most considerable respect, and the expression of the warmest love from him who is, and ever shall be, paper without end, A man (*qui est réussi*)

S.O.B.

Theirs was an ideally happy domestic and literary partnership, to which nearly a decade of hard work had now brought an honourable success. It is worth while reviewing this success in more detail, while as yet it is unclouded by the shadows of impending tragedy and misfortune.

II

As Beeton's publishing business grew he found it necessary to move to larger offices; and so early in 1860, as already related, the offices in Bouverie Street had been exchanged for new premises at 248 Strand, on the site of the present Law Courts, "10 doors from Temple Bar," as he proudly advertised on his notepaper. These accommodated the successful publisher and editor at the height of his prosperity.

The work which he undertook was prodigious and taxed his physical resources to the utmost. Indeed, it was too much for any one man; and had he not been overwhelmed by misfortune and catastrophe when he was, it is doubtful whether he could have kept it up much longer than he did. In addition to several hundred books that were issued from his offices, he published and edited no fewer than seven periodicals and was closely associated with an eighth. His principal aim, as we have seen, was to satisfy the needs of the young folk and women of the country with suitable periodical literature. The seven works which he edited, and which always had this aim in view, were, in the order of their foundation: *The Englishwoman's Domestic Magazine*, *The Boy's Own Magazine*, *The Boy's Monthly Magazine*, *The Boy's Penny Magazine*, *Beeton's Christmas Annual*, *The Queen*, and *The Young Englishwoman*. In addition he was concerned with the first cheap sporting newspaper, *The Sporting Life*.

The Sporting Life, which may be mentioned here, made

its appearance in Fleet Street in rather peculiar circumstances in 1859. It is known that S. O. Beeton had a hand
in its first production, but how far, if at all, he was connected with its subsequent conduct and policy is uncertain.
His original connexion is easily explained when his family
association with Epsom Races is borne in mind—the fact
that it was at his father's suggestion some years previously
that the Great Metropolitan Stakes had been started, and
the fact that his mother-in-law was married to the Clerk
of the Course. The promoter of the paper was George
Maddick, a well-known journalist, who was advised by
several friends, including S. O. Beeton, to establish a cheap
sporting paper, since the only journal which catered for
this class of reader was *Bell's Life in London*, a highly priced
weekly. The paper was accordingly arranged to appear
three times a week, and its original title was *The Penny
Bell's Life, or Sporting News*.

The proprietors of the older paper, not unnaturally,
objected to what they considered to be an illegitimate
appropriation of their title. Legal action was taken, but
fortunately in the litigation which followed a solution to
the difficulty was found. Curiously enough it came from
the Bench. "Why can't you call it *The Sporting Life*?"
said the judge who tried the case to defendant's counsel.
The suggestion was immediately adopted, and, while
many publications have lost their title through decision
from the Bench, this is a rare case where one was gained.
The new journal proved an immediate success, and ultimately incorporated its old rival, *Bell's Life*.

The rapid extension of Beeton's publishing activities
was considerably helped by an important event which
took place in 1861, and which had been foreshadowed

some years previously. This was the repeal of the Paper Duty, the last of the so-called "taxes on knowledge." The obnoxious newspaper stamp had disappeared in 1853, but the duty on paper still remained a serious obstacle to a cheap Press. The manner in which this obstacle was finally removed is remarkable. The House of Lords declared its intention of opposing the measure of repeal to the last ditch. They accordingly threw out the Bill after it had passed through the Commons in 1860. The Chancellor of the Exchequer, Mr Gladstone, thereupon decided to embody the measure in his Budget for the following year; and the Lords, who had the right to reject but not to amend a financial measure, were reluctantly obliged to pass it, rather than run the risk of raising a storm by throwing out the whole budget. Gladstone's tactics, though strongly questioned on constitutional grounds, were therefore completely successful.

Owing to the delay in passing the measure, however, many publishers who had been counting on the remission of the duty suffered financial loss. Among these was S. O. Beeton, who, as we have seen, commenced a new and much enlarged series of *The Englishwoman's Domestic Magazine* in the spring of 1860, in the confident expectation that the duty would immediately be repealed, and during the ensuing eighteen months that the duty continued in operation he was obliged to pay in taxes on paper and plates used for that journal a sum upward of £1000. Even greater improvements were possible when the duty was taken off. "Although then," he wrote at the time,

> we thus anticipated the reduction in the price of paper and did not abate one tittle of quality or quantity, we shall still give in various ways to our subscribers all the advantages

which may accrue to us. A superior quality of paper will
be employed in printing the Magazine, and we shall be able
to dispense larger sums to our authors, designers, engravers,
and printers, with the usual result, it is hoped, of getting
better work from all.

The Englishwoman's Domestic Magazine had now a
circulation of over 60,000 copies a month. In a leading
article on "Mr Beeton's Publications" which appeared in
The Standard in 1863 this journal was given pride of place.
It was described as "a wonderful publication in size, in
matter, and above all in price."

It is but sixpence, and for that tiny coin Mr Beeton pro-
vides forty-eight pages of excellent matter, an engraving or
two generally from the pencil of Miss Florence Claxton, and
plate of fashions, one or two coloured designs for work,
and a large sheet full on one side of engravings of work
and on the other side outlines of the newest fashions; so that
ladies may, if they please, have their dresses made up at
home by a girl 'coming in.' We have the authority of
'Materfamilias' for saying that the house would go to sixes
and sevens if the magazine failed to put in its monthly
appearance.[1]

The paper patterns, which immediately caught the public
fancy, have already been mentioned as forming a conspicuous feature of the first series. Coloured fashion plates
were another novelty which *The Englishwoman's Domestic
Magazine* was the first journal in England to issue to its
readers. The plates were designed by a Frenchman, Jules
David, and engraved in Paris to the order of the French
publisher Adolphe Goubaud, who conducted a leading
Paris fashion publication called *Le Moniteur de la Mode*,

[1] *The Standard*, January 25, 1863.

and with whom, as we have seen, Beeton entered into an arrangement to have the use of the plates for his own publications. As before, Mrs Beeton edited the columns on "The Fashions," and regularly journeyed to Paris twice a year to study and bring back the latest models in spring and autumn.

The success of *The Englishwoman's Domestic Magazine*, which was due in great measure to these features, encouraged the publisher to bring out a weekly journal on similar lines. It was to be the same price as the monthly—namely, sixpence—but the size was to be folio instead of octavo, so as to make it uniform with the other leading illustrated weeklies of the time. A prominent feature was to be the news of the week, which, the editor promised, would "be narrated in decent English and without the excessive verbiage which disfigures so many existing journals." The events of the day were illustrated by engravings "to give point to whatever topics happen to engage the public mind." The paper was to be called *The Queen*, and in this style it accordingly made its first appearance on September 7, 1861. A photograph of her Majesty Queen Victoria, "elegantly mounted on tinted cardpaper," was included with every copy of this first number.

As editor of *The Queen*, Beeton secured the services of his old friend Frederick Greenwood, an elder brother of James Greenwood and an exceptionally able journalist, who was later to edit the *Pall Mall Gazette* with conspicuous success, and who deserves honourable mention for having suggested to Disraeli the purchase by the British Government of the shares in the Suez Canal Company, for which that statesmen received the credit. The son of

a coach-upholsterer in Kensington, Greenwood began life
as a printer's devil and compositor, at which he worked for
sixteen hours a day. He later became a publisher's reader,
and it will be remembered that he first met Beeton at the
time of the publication of *Uncle Tom's Cabin*, when he
was consulted about this project. His niece Mrs Maria
Robinson, who lived to the age of 103, lately used to recall
meeting Samuel and Isabella Beeton at the Greenwoods'
house in Islington, along with W. B. Rands, J. G. Edgar,
and other contributors to the various Beeton publications.
Sam Beeton she described as "a very nice gentleman,"
while Isabella was "a good practical cook, very lively and
chatty, and something of a practical joker." According to
Mrs Robinson, the wives of some of her friends complained that their husbands came home and said, "Why
can't you cook like Mrs Beeton?" Consequently at the
next gathering at her house to which the husbands were
invited Isabella "dished up a shocking meal in order to
teach the men not to criticize their wives."

The Queen rapidly fulfilled public expectations. Its
sixteen pages covered every field of women's interests, as
well as the principal items of news. "We have attempted
to redeem our promise," wrote the editor when the paper
had been in circulation for some seven months,

> that we should make it a perfect Lady's Journal. Such a
> Journal has never before been provided for the ladies of this
> country, though some have attempted the task. The pro-
> blem which we have set ourselves to the solution of is, how
> to provide a weekly Record and Journal which ladies can
> read and profit by; one in which their understandings and
> judgments will not be insulted by a collection of mere
> trivialities, but which will be to them a help in their daily

lives and which will provide them with just that information which they require.[1]

Dress and needlework supplements were regularly inserted in *The Queen*, and, as in the case of *The English-woman's Domestic Magazine*, Isabella wrote the fashion articles. These included a description of the dresses shown each week in the coloured fashion plate, which was as prominent a feature in *The Queen* as in the sister journal.

Samuel Beeton was, however, not yet satisfied. He was determined to found another woman's journal, which would do for young ladies what his various boys' publications had done for the youth of the country. The result was *The Young Englishwoman*, which was first published in December 1864. It was described in the original prospectus as "a new Magazine of Fiction and Entertaining Literature, Music, Poetry, the Fine Arts, the Fashions, and Useful and Ornamental Needlework." Anxious parents and guardians were assured that "it may be placed without the slightest fear in the hands of girls of tender age." The first number contained thirty-two pages, "a charming Picture after W. L. Thomas called 'Minding Baby,' and a supplementary sheet of designs and patterns." The price of this amazing production was only a penny, and it was on sale once a week. A useful band of contributors was enlisted, including T. W. Robertson, whose novel *David Garrick*, later converted into the well-known play of the same name, commenced to appear serially with the first number. Tom Robertson also wrote the dramatic notes for *The Queen*.

Meanwhile the boys' publications were pursuing their way merrily and continued to increase their circulation.

[1] *The Queen*, April 12, 1862.

The Boy's Own Magazine, which now contained ninety-six pages for sixpence, had over 40,000 readers. The prize competitions had a good deal to do with this popularity, and among other rewards in the shape of gold and silver watches, pencil-cases, and chemical chests were distributed "one thousand of the best finished knives with buckthorn handles, containing various blades, tweezers, corkscrews, &c. of the full guaranteed value of 8s. 6d. each." The increase in price from 2d. to 6d. necessitated by these attractions induced the editor to found *The Boy's Penny Magazine*, since it was represented to him that this increase would prevent some boys from buying the elder periodical. It was later incorporated in *The Boy's Monthly Magazine*. In addition he published twice yearly a *Boy's Annual* containing the best contributions to the weekly and monthly publications as well as new stories. The authors who wrote for these magazines included Captain Mayne Reid, Clement Scott, W. B. Rands, Tom Hood the younger, W. H. Davenport Adams, and James Greenwood. They were illustrated by such artists as Gustave Doré, L. C. Henley, Gordon Thomson, and Harrison Weir.

Béranger's claim upon the love of his countrymen was that he had written the songs they sang. Beeton's was that he had edited and published the books that boys read. "I would not enter on my list of friends him who thought lightly of the business of 'Cater' for the boy's mess," he wrote, with this comparison in mind at the end of ten years of this work,

> and should dearly love to see the writhings of the man who thought the thing easy, when he had seated himself on the cushion, for the thorns of which I can very well vouch, having felt them more than a decade of years, and remem-

bering their pricks the more that when I began to sit in that same seat I was young, and, thereupon, tender. So I will not plead guilty to my harsh critic, who declares that the mere editor and writer for a few lads in this present age is impertinent and egotistical when he has the hardihood to refer to any sort of coincidence between a great poet and a little publisher. No, I answer, love ennobles all work, and I love mine; and if I sell my books—and I devoutly hope many *will* continue to be sold—so did Béranger, not to speak of our own Laureate, sell his verses for the benefit of himself and the people.

In addition to the *Household Management* and *Dictionary of Universal Information*, which have already been mentioned, a number of other *Beeton's Books* were published at this time, most of them appearing first in monthly parts. They covered such subjects as *Universal Biography*, *Poetry*, *Games*, *Chemistry*, *Home Pets*, *Poultry and Domestic Animals*, *Birds and Garden Management*. As he remarked some years later, "the originator of this series of compendious Cyclopædias has been aided by a number of honest workers, who have very diligently sought to carry out faithfully and fully the first idea of these works which was that they should be thoroughly good books, serviceable and useful to the community at large." Classics like *Robinson Crusoe*, *Gulliver's Travels*, *Don Quixote*, and Motley's *Dutch Republic* were published in a form suitable for youthful consumption, and the works of American humourists such as "Artemus Ward" and "Petroleum V. Nasby" were introduced to the public through the offices of 248 Strand. The only venture which did not prove successful was *Beeton's Illuminated Family Bible*. This was a conscientious attempt to present the Scriptures in a form humanly worthy of their authorship and object at a price varying between three and four guineas, in accordance with the style of binding. No pains were spared in getting up the letterpress and engaging the best artists of Biblical subjects to contribute illustrations. The result was the "beautiful enshrinement" of Holy Writ, profusely illustrated and handsomely bound, but unfortunately the Bible did not attract the public in this dress, and the publisher was to suffer heavy losses on its account.

Finally, there was *Beeton's Christmas Annual*, which was, taken all in all, perhaps the most successful of the Beeton periodical publications. The first number was published in 1860, and contained, in the words of one advertisement, "100 large pages, beautifully printed and illustrated, with a most handsome Eidographic Almanac in Gold and Colours."

> The contents are Tales, Essays, Fables, Biography, History, Ballads, Songs, Sketches, Adventures, Romances, Dreams, Fancies, Philosophy, Natural History, and a Large Separate Sheet of Puzzles, a Christmas Burlesque to be acted by members of the Home Circle; a host of Christmas Games, Sports, Pastimes, Puzzles, Riddles, Conundrums and the like; besides the more useful accompaniments of a Household Almanac . . . Price, with Key to the Puzzles, 1s. 3d.

Among the earlier contributors was numbered F. C. Burnand, later Sir Francis Burnand and editor of *Punch*. The names of George Cruikshank Junior, Thomas Archer, C. H. Bennett, W. Blanchard, J. C. Brough, Thomas Hood the younger, and W. B. Rands were also "featured" regularly. As we shall see, the general character of the *Christmas Annuals* was not always to remain the same, but the earlier numbers contained no hint of the radical change which was to come before Beeton's association with the publication ceased.

The offices at 248 Strand were a veritable hive of industry in these years, and more than justified the "Sign of the Bee-hive" which the publisher had adopted as a trademark. And this industry brought its own reward in the shape of fame as a publisher, handsome profits, and domestic happiness. In the words of the *Standard* leader in praise of the Beeton publications, "Mr Beeton is doing a great work in our national education, and public appreciation gives him its reward." The dawn of the year 1865, therefore, found him well established and highly successful in his business. Little did he anticipate then the series of cruel blows of Fate which were to rob him first of his domestic happiness and secondly of his fortune and goodwill as a publisher.

III

Christmas 1864 was spent in their new house, at Greenhithe, awaiting the happy event to which both parents were looking forward. Although the first two children born to them had died, the third, who had appeared in the previous year and whom they called Orchart, was a thoroughly healthy baby; and the next, they hoped, would entirely compensate them for the earlier loss. As their friend and neighbour Mrs Browne put it, "they were so anxious to have two little boys playing together."

Isabella was kept busy up to the time of her confinement revising and correcting the proofs of the *Dictionary of*

Every-day Cookery, a shortened version of the *Household Management* which contained the principal recipes. After her death there seems to have been a good deal of family gossip to the effect that she did too much at this period, and even that her husband "killed her" with worry about business affairs. But there would appear to be little or no substance to these tales. She was a strong, healthy young woman, who had never had a day's illness in her life, and it is doubtful whether her activities at Greenhithe and her trips to the office in London contributed in any measure to the tragedy which followed.

On January 29, 1865, Isabella Beeton gave birth to a son. At first she seemed to be doing well, but next day she suddenly developed puerperal fever. Thanks largely to the work of two great men, the Hungarian physician Semmelweiss and the English surgeon Lister, we now know that this infection was caused by deliveries taking place without aseptic precautions. But their work had not become known and accepted at this time, and, so far as Isabella Beeton was concerned, it is highly probable that the doctor and midwife who attended her did not take any of those precautions to prevent sepsis which are now regarded as a commonplace in maternity cases. Had her confinement taken place to-day, the outcome would almost certainly have been different. Unfortunately, as things were, the fever did not pass. The patient grew steadily worse, and a week later, on February 6, she died. Had she lived for a few weeks longer, she would have completed her twenty-ninth year.

The blow which deprived Samuel Beeton of a wonderful wife and a valued literary helper was all the more severe in that it was entirely unexpected. The following

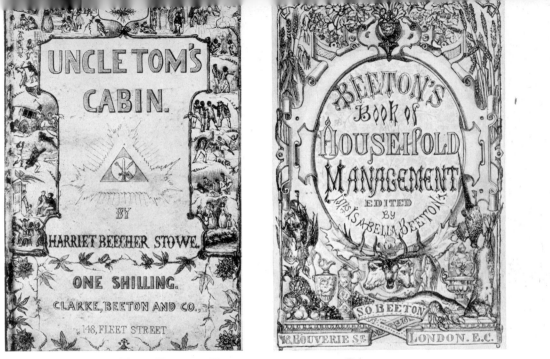

Two Famous Books published by Beeton

The cover of the first English edition
of *Uncle Tom's Cabin*, published in
1852.
[*See pp*. 33–44.]

The title-page of the first edition
of Mrs Beeton's famous book, first
published in 1861, having previously
appeared in twenty-four monthly parts.

S. O. BEETON'S PUBLISHING OFFICES AT 248 STRAND

These offices were on the site of the present Law Courts. Temple Bar, later removed, can be seen on the right.

From a contemporary engraving

letter, which he wrote to his uncle-by-marriage, William Stagg,[1] shows how deeply he was affected.

GREENHITHE,
Feb. 18, '65

MY DEAR, GOOD MR STAGG,

I can hardly write a word to you that has reference to the great blow that it has pleased Heaven to strike me. I am able to attend to my business matters, and am, although exhausted in body, not worse in health than usual.

My Orchy is well, very well—looking more like a child of yours than of mine—he is so fat and ruddy. And the little one—whom I shall call Mayson—is thriving under a very good nurse we found for him who had a little girl 6 weeks old. So, if I keep *her* two children, dear Stagg, it will be something for me.

To tell you all: my agony is excessive, but I have hours of calm and quiet which refresh me and enable me to meet the dreadful grief that well nigh overpowers me, and renders me unable to move or stir. But I hope to conquer at last, and will strive, with all the courage I have and can receive by appeals to her good spirit, and to the All-Ruler, to live a good life, honest and pure, to hold the love and respect of good men, and not lose my self-respect. In doing this, and in trying to bring up my two little ones, I shall obtain, I think, some comfort.

Tell me in a day or two how yr. darling wife is (oh! how Bella reverenced her!) and when she is able, she will write me a few of her kind lines. I have so yearned to see yr. face and press yr. hand, and was so glad to get yr. two notes.

All have been to me very good, here and in London, and

---

[1] William Stagg married Thomasin, daughter of Samuel Beeton, the original proprietor of The Dolphin.

one strain only can be heard of respect and love for her memory.

God bless you ever—and yours:

and Believe me Affty. yr.

S.O.B.

P.S. At the latter end of next week I go to Paris, to one of my best friends and best of men—Monsieur Goubaud. I have a great deal of business there, much of which was done by *her*. Then I go to young Mayson Dorling's, Forest Hill, where Orchy is, for a day or two, and return here with my child. The little one is within 5 minutes' walk of this.

In more formal but no less touching language S. O. Beeton wrote a vivid obituary notice of his wife. It was hastily added as an Epilogue to *Mrs Beeton's Dictionary of Every-day Cookery*, the last work on which they were engaged together, and which appeared early in 1865.

USQUE AD FINEM

Her Hand has lost its cunning—the firm true hand that wrote these formulæ and penned the information contained in this little book. Cold in the silent tomb lie the once nimble, useful fingers—now nerveless, unable for anything, and ne'er to do work more in this world. Exquisite palate, unerring judgment, sound common sense, refined tastes— all these had the dear lady who has gone 'ere her youth had scarcely come. But four times seven years were all she passed in this world; and since the day she became wedded wife—now nearly nine years passed—her greatest, chiefest aims were to provide for the comfort and pleasure of those she loved and had around her, and to employ her best faculties for the use of her sisters, Englishwomen generally. Her surpassing affection and devotion led her to find happiness in aiding, with all her heart and soul, the Husband whom she richly blessed and honoured with her abounding love.

Her Works speak for themselves; and, although taken from this world in the very height of health and strength, and in the early days of womanhood, she felt that satisfaction—so great to all who strive with good intent and warm will—of knowing herself regarded with respect and gratitude.

Her labours are ended here; in purer atmosphere she dwells; and maybe in the land beyond the skies, she has a nobler work to accomplish. Her plans for the future cannot be wholly carried out; her husband knew them all, and will diligently devote himself to their execution, as far as may be. The remembrance of her wishes—always for the private and public welfare—and the companionship of her two little boys—too young to know the virtues of their good Mother —this memory, this presence, will nerve the Father, left alone, to continue to do his duty; in which he will follow the example of his Wife, for her duty no woman has ever better accomplished than the late

ISABELLA MARY BEETON

IV

It was only when Samuel Beeton took up the threads of his work, thus rudely broken, that he realized to the full how much he depended upon his wife for her assistance and collaboration. The friendly nurse whom he had found at Greenhithe, Mrs Moss, took charge of the two children, but the gap at the work-table could not be filled so easily. The publisher endeavoured to do this in his own person, but, rather than run the chance of breaking down under the additional strain, he decided to dispose of one of his magazines, and fixed on *The Queen*. This journal now passed to Horace Cox, a member of the firm of Cox and Wyman, who had printed it; and it remained until recently in the possession of the Cox family. Beeton continued, however, to produce the other periodicals which he had founded, being considerably helped in the editorial room by three trusty colleagues—the Rev. J. G. Wood, John Tillotson, and Francis Young. He had now to look after the Paris end of the business, which had been one of Isabella's particular interests. We accordingly find him in the French capital soon after her death, and again in the summer of 1865, when her half-sister Lucy, who was on her way to school, recalls what a knowledgeable and painstaking guide he was, driving round in a little victoria and showing her the sights.

Shortly after this S. O. Beeton made his first appearance in a locality which was to become unpleasantly familiar to him some years later. This was the Court of Chancery, which in those days, before the building of the present Law Courts, sat in Westminster Hall. The dispute arose over the reprint by Beeton of a book by the American humorist Artemus Ward. The work in question had already appeared in England under the imprint of another publisher, but the latter fondly imagined, in face of the fact that the law of international copyright did not prevent English publishers reprinting the works of American authors at discretion, that his copyright was being infringed. The rival publisher applied to the Chancery Court for an injunction to restrain Beeton from publishing his version, and the judge to whom the application was made very properly refused it. "I might," remarked Beeton at the time, "being the original publisher of *Uncle Tom*, as well have applied to restrain the publication of the dozens of reprints of that remarkable book." Nevertheless he strongly advocated the reform of the copyright laws, which he aptly described as being "fog and confusion," particularly in view of the fact that no agreement as yet existed between Great Britain and the United States for the mutual protection of their copyrights.

Samuel Beeton worked harder than ever now, and in increased literary activities he sought to forget his great grief. Matters, however, did not go so well as formerly. For one thing, his health began to give trouble. He tired easily, and developed an irritating cough, whose sound was ominous. Consumption was getting its deadly grip upon him. Neither was business so good. True, there was no appreciable falling off in the circulation of the various magazines, and the *Household Management* was selling as well as ever, but he was obliged to meet the heavy losses incurred by the ill-fated *Beeton's Illuminated Family Bible*, which had cost a considerable sum to produce and had sold very badly. In ordinary circumstances he could easily have borne the loss out of past profits, but there now occurred a catastrophic event, which not only made it impossible for him to meet this loss alone, but involved him and all his literary undertaking in financial ruin. This event was the failure of the great banking house of Overend, Gurney and Co. on May 10, 1866. It claimed S. O. Beeton among its numerous victims.

Never had such a panic been known in Lombard Street since that Friday in December 1745 when the news that Bonnie Prince Charlie was marching on London was received in the City. Like the earlier occasion, the day after Overend, Gurney, and Co. suspended payment and

put up its shutters came to be known as "Black Friday."
It was probably the worst crisis ever experienced in the
City of London. *The Times* described the bank's failure
as "a national calamity." Theirs was the largest discount
house in the country, and their liabilities were in the region
of £20 millions. What had happened was that the rapid
improvement in trade and industry generally during the
previous few years had been followed by the usual speculation and overtrading. The recent creation of numerous
joint-stock companies with "limited liability"—Overend,
Gurney, and Co. themselves had recently been incorporated in this style—increased the tendency towards inflation.
Unfortunately, attracted by the prevailing high rates of
interest, Overend, Gurney, and Co. began to discount
bills of questionable security. When the slump came they
consequently went down and brought numerous small
depositors with them. Beeton himself had also over-
traded in his business.

Bankruptcy stared the publisher in the face, and to avoid
this pit there was nothing left for him but to seize any
opportunity offered by his creditors for satisfying their
demands. Petitions were threatened, but happily none
was ever filed in Carey Street, and Samuel Beeton was
consequently never adjudicated a bankrupt, since he
entered into a composition with his creditors. The publishing firm of Ward, Lock, and Tyler came forward with
an offer that Beeton should dispose of the copyrights in
his various publications to them and become their salaried
literary adviser. The offer was accepted, for Beeton could
not well do otherwise; but its terms, as we shall shortly
see, were onerous and were bound to lead ultimately to
friction between the parties. It must have been a cruel

wrench to give up the old offices at 248 Strand, through whose doors his most successful publications had issued; but at least he entered those of Ward, Lock, and Tyler in Paternoster Row in a spirit of hope for the future and gratitude that he was now in a position to pay off his debts.

With this object in view it had previously been arranged that Ward, Lock, and Tyler should act as Beeton's trustees and administer his property until his debts were discharged. The terms by which it was eventually agreed that Beeton should join this firm took some months to negotiate. Lock thought that he was asking for too large a share of the future profits from the sale of the Beeton publications. "I'm not much of a bargainer, although you think I am," Beeton told Lock at this time. "I only want to be 'settled' and my future dependent on the moneys I aid in making, so I should be satisfied with one-third of the nett results as shown by the profits arising from the estate of S.O.B."

At last the contract was agreed between the parties and signed. It cannot be described as over-generous. Beeton was to receive a salary of £400 a year and one-sixth of the profits, though the share of the profits was to rise yearly to one-fifth, and finally to a quarter. "He was very good about it," said a friend afterwards. "Never a grumble."

No change was made in the style of any of the Beeton publications, except that the name of Ward, Lock, and Tyler now appeared as the publishers. Beeton remained in control of this side of the business, and, at first at any rate, seems to have been given a free hand in the choice of assistants. Many of the old contributors continued to give their services under the new régime, but fresh blood was also utilized. A valued helper at this time was C. E.

Weldon, later the founder of the well-known series of fashion journals which bore his name. But particularly fortunate was Beeton in securing an exceptionally able woman as literary collaborator and editress of *The English-woman's Domestic Magazine* and *The Young Englishwoman*, very shortly after he had commenced work with Ward, Lock, and Tyler. This was Mrs Matilda Browne, who, with her husband, C. R. Browne, of the Westminster Fire Office, lived near Beeton's house at Greenhithe. The daughter of a solicitor named Walls, she was born in the same year as Mrs Beeton. Her father, who had served beside Prince Louis Napoleon as a special constable during the Chartist agitation of 1848, had taken her to the French capital as the guest of the Emperor Napoleon III, so that she had seen Paris and its fashions long before she came to visit it as editress of *The Englishwoman's Domestic Magazine* and *The Young Englishwoman*. Previously an occasional contributor to these publications, she had shown herself an apt journalist, and now she was able to help S. O. Beeton in their management much in the same way as his wife had done.[1]

What is more, the two families agreed to "put their two poverties together," and the Brownes moved into the rambling house at Greenhithe. However, they found Mount Pleasant too costly an establishment to maintain, and they soon migrated to a cottage at the top of the hill above the village. This cottage was an extension of the old Coast Guard preventive station, and here the two families kept a joint household for the next seven years. Besides housekeeping, Mrs Browne also assumed responsibility for the upbringing of the two young Beeton

[1] She died on April 24, 1936, in her hundredth year.

children, who, as they grew up, came to regard her as their own mother.

An interesting publication which Beeton prepared and edited at this time was a slim folio volume entitled *London's Great Outing: The Derby Carnival*. It described in detail the classic race at Epsom and the varied scenes on the Downs, and was illustrated by some excellent woodcut engravings of sketches by "Phiz." It also contained a sharp dig at his stepfather-in-law, Henry Dorling, who occupied the all-important positions of Clerk of the Course and owner of the Grand Stand. Here is an extract from what he wrote; it suggests that by now there can have been little love lost between the two families:

> To any man who is really fond of a horse, and likes to see the animals that are about to contend for the Blue Riband, let me commend to him, above all and before all on the course, a visit to the paddock. There appears to be some idea in the public mind that there is some occult difficulty in getting into this charming enclosure at Epsom, belonging to Arthur Heathcote. Half-a-sovereign is the difficulty—that is all. Indeed, you may take it as a certainty that for money at Epsom all things are possible. The Clerk of the Course has studied too closely for one-and-twenty years the art of filling his pockets from every available source, and is too fond of the red gold not to make everything that he has any control over quite easy to purchase. Ready, ay ready, to sell anybody or anything—that's the family motto.

At the beginning of 1869 Beeton took over the publication on his own account of *The Weekly Despatch*, then a leading Liberal organ. In this he was particularly assisted by Weldon, who eventually undertook the whole work

himself. One of the few of Beeton's letters of this time
which have survived concerns the right to publish the paper
on Sunday. It is written to his old friend Frederick
Weaklin.

"WEEKLY DESPATCH,"
139 FLEET STREET,
March 25, '69

MY DEAR SIR,

You can do me a great turn. You are powerful in the
Vestry of St Bride's I hear; and we want a right to publish
the *Dispatch* on Sunday morning, all work to be over by
11 o'clock, and the place shut. In Alderman Harmer's
time, there used to be a lot of queer-looking fellows employed to shout out "Latest Murder" etc., in Fleet St., wh.
cries were not very edifying, I dare say, or interesting to
Church goers.

But all that is altered now—we begin to publish at 4 o'c
in the morning, and all can be over at 10 or 11, as I have said.

We have applied in an official sort of way to the Parish
Authorities to alter that portion of the Lease wh. prevents
us from making any use of the place on Sunday morning,
but are told they cannot interfere.

Will you kindly consider the case, and advise me how
to act.

Yours very truly,
S. O. BEETON

The matter, which was of considerable consequence to
the publisher, seems to have ended satisfactorily. "It will
be a very serious advantage to us to carry our point,"
wrote Beeton in a letter thanking Weaklin for his help,
"and for the Sunday part of the business, it is all over
before the day begins, Monday's papers want Sunday
work—not Sunday's."

Meanwhile, for various reasons, friction was increasing between S. O. Beeton and the firm of publishers who now employed him. He had never before been an employee, and he was not the type of man who could work with any individual or concern where he was not the master. As the breach widened between them it gradually became clear that their differences would have to be settled by law.

V

The chief cause of the dispute between S. O. Beeton and the firm of Ward, Lock, and Tyler was provided by *Beeton's Christmas Annual*, whose copyright the publishers had acquired along with the rest of the Beeton publications. It had been founded in 1860, when Beeton was, perhaps, at the height of his success, and, though now no longer the owner, he continued to edit it as the publication of Ward, Lock, and Tyler. Down to 1871 the annual retained its original features of seasonable fiction, history burlesques, games, and other things suitable for the fireside at Christmas. In the following year, however, Beeton, who had always been a staunch Radical, conceived the idea of throwing over most of these items and substituting a piece of political satire parodying the work of some well-known author, and fiercely backing Gladstone and the Radicals against Disraeli and the Conservatives. Accordingly, along with two collaborators, A. A. Dowty, of the Paymaster-General's office, and a journalist named S. R. Emerson, he executed it under the title of *The Coming K——*. This work, which was composed in the style of Tennyson's *Idylls of the King*, severely criticized the vices and follies of the age, and particularly the private

life of the Prince of Wales and the social set in which he
moved. The *Annual* had an immediate success, and created
a sensation in the fashionable world of London. In spite
of this, however, Messrs Ward and Lock, who had not
seen the *Annual* in MS., strongly disapproved of its contents, reprimanded the editor, and refused to publish a
second edition.

The following year's *Annual*, which was called *The
Siliad* and was the work of the same authors, pleased Ward
and Lock no better than *The Coming K——*. As it had
been left too late to prepare a substitute, Ward and Lock
were reluctantly obliged to publish it. However, they
determined that the character and contents of the next
volume must be drastically altered, and they told Beeton
so. Their demand was considerably strengthened by the
retirement from the firm at this time of the third partner,
Mr Charles Tyler, who was a friend of Beeton's and had
always taken his part against the others. Accordingly,
when Beeton submitted his plan for the Annual for 1874,
which he proposed to call *Jon Duan* and which was
designed as a continuation of *The Coming K——* and
The Siliad, Ward and Lock summarily turned it down.
They thereupon entrusted the preparation of the *Annual*
to Emerson, who produced a volume entitled *The Fijiad*,
which appeared as *Beeton's Christmas Annual* for that year,
but in whose composition the original editor had no share.
But, as Beeton had expended considerable labour on his
annual along with his two collaborators, A. A. Dowty and
Evelyn Jerrold, son of the author Blanchard Jerrold, who
had taken Emerson's place, he made up his mind that it
should be published, and it was, in fact, brought out by
his old colleague C. E. Weldon, who had now set up as a

publisher on his own account. Since, however, it was advertised as having been devised by S. O. Beeton while *Beeton's Christmas Annual* was already in the press, Ward, Lock, and Co. applied to the Court of Chancery for an injunction to restrain the advertisement of the rival work. The case was heard before Vice-Chancellor Sir Richard Malins in November and December 1874, and ended in a judgment for the plaintiffs.

Beeton's defence was that Ward, Lock had been wrongly informed that he was engaged in getting up a Christmas Annual *in opposition to them*. On the contrary, it was he who had reason to complain of their conduct. He had some months before informed Mr Lock of the whole plan he had arranged for the *Annual* of 1874, and both Mr Lock and Mr Ward had refused to publish it. But, he contended, as he could not under his agreement produce a Christmas Annual elsewhere, all the suggestions and plans which were a material part of the publication became the property of the authors of the two previous *Annuals*, of which this one (*Jon Duan*) was to be the continuation; and these authors (Dowty and Jerrold), being his friends and unacquainted with publishing, had asked his advice in many things, and he could not refuse to help them; that he had at their request given instructions in connexion with it, but there was nothing in his conduct inconsistent with his agreement with Messrs Ward and Lock. He had merely assisted his friends with his advice, but he denied having entered into any arrangement with them as to sharing profits and losses.

The Vice-Chancellor, however, ruled that Beeton's action in recommending what must from its nature be considered as a rival publication constituted a breach of duty as between servant and employer, and he accordingly granted Ward, Lock the injunction sought for. Briefly the burden of his judgment was that, since the plaintiffs had purchased the copyright of and the right to use the name of the defendant in the publication of the work known as *Beeton's Christmas Annual*, and since the defendant had agreed to give his whole time to the service of the plaintiffs, and not to engage in any other business without their consent, the defendant must be restrained from advertising a rival work. By acting as he had done Beeton had unfortunately taken the law into his own hands. "If he thought he had a case," observed the judge, *à propos* of Beeton's feelings towards Ward, Lock,

> he ought to have filed a bill to restrain them from publishing that work with his name when he had nothing to do with it: but he took the law into his own hands, and issued the advertisements which are calculated most materially to injure the Plaintiffs, and according to his statement it could do him no good except to gratify his vanity.

On the question of Ward, Lock's right to use Beeton's name in connexion with the *Christmas Annual*, the Vice-Chancellor stated the law in what is perhaps the most revealing part of his judgment:

> What is the meaning of purchasing *Beeton's Christmas Annual*? Did it mean that they could not call it "Beeton's Annual" unless Beeton superintended the publication of it or approved of the contents? It would have been just the same if they had bought *Blackwood's Magazine* or *Frazer's Magazine* or any publication known by a particular name. It does not certainly mean that the person whose name it has borne is to continue to be connected with it, and I take

it to be perfectly clear that when they bought all the copyright, they bought all the property, copyright, and so forth constituting the property of Beeton; and it is perfectly clear in my mind that they acquired the right to publish this publication as *Beeton's Annual*, although Beeton might not have continued to have any connection with it whatever. He was a party to that sale, either he or his creditors or his assignee, and nothing can be more unfounded than the contention that selling a periodical publication means only the one number of it. It means the continuance of that thing known as an annual, or a monthly or daily publication, as the case may be. When you sell a newspaper it is not merely the right to sell one number of it, but continuing to publish it from day to day, it may be as long as the world lasts, under the name by which it became known; therefore, I am of opinion that the sale of this copyright in 1866 gave the Plaintiffs the right to publish it, although Mr Beeton ceased to have any connection with it.

With the granting of this injunction Beeton's contract of service with Ward, Lock was dissolved, and he was free once more to start publishing on his own. But the strain and worry of the lawsuit had taken a heavy toll of his failing health, and to avoid a complete breakdown his doctor ordered him abroad for a rest.

Chapter VI

THE REPUBLICAN MOVEMENT

THE most casual student of English political history cannot fail to be struck by the change in the popular attitude towards the monarchy which has taken place during the century following the death of George IV. When this sovereign died in 1830 *The Times* came out with the bald statement that "there never was an individual less regretted by his fellow creatures than this deceased King." Such an expression of feeling is in strong contrast with the spontaneous outburst of national grief which occurred throughout the whole British Empire on the death of His Majesty King George V in 1935.

While the prestige of the Crown has increased enormously since Regency days, its power has suffered a corresponding decline. However, recent research has shown that the diminution of royal prerogative was not as great in the reign of Queen Victoria as certain acknowledged constitutional authorities have supposed. It is not proposed here to follow this process throughout the century, but rather one phase of it, in which S. O. Beeton was definitely involved through his *Christmas Annual*. This phase was the so-called Republican craze of the seventies, and it marks perhaps the height of the Queen's personal unpopularity with her subjects.

The public attitude to the throne in the long reign of the nineteenth century was by no means as loyal and enthusi-

S. O. BEETON
Aged about forty.
From a contemporary photograph

144

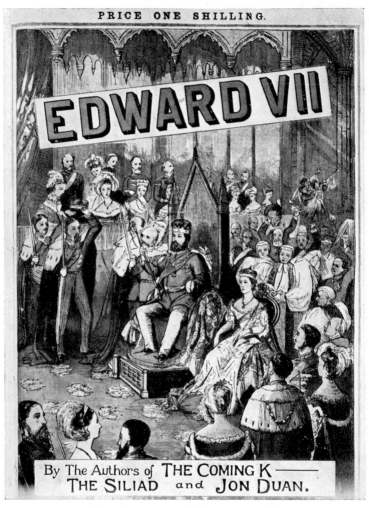

PRICE ONE SHILLING.

EDWARD VII

By The Authors of THE COMING K——
THE SILIAD and JON DUAN.

THE COVER OF "EDWARD VII"

This was the last of Beeton's *Christmas Annuals*. It appeared
in 1876.

astic as was reflected towards its close in the two Jubilees. The Queen certainly commenced her reign with the friendship and goodwill of her people. For various reasons she lost this esteem; and, though she more than regained it before the end of the reign, at the period with which we are immediately concerned she was the subject of repeated attack in the Radical Press to such an extent that rumours of her abdication were current. The principal cause of her unpopularity was the long spell of strict seclusion which she willingly underwent in consequence of the death of her beloved Consort Prince Albert. Her life during several years was spent between Windsor, Osborne, and Balmoral; she was only visible to a fraction of her subjects; and her appearances in London were rare and reluctant. Furthermore, she spent little money, which was generally felt to be bad for trade. The predominant German influences at Court were partly blamed for the Queen's conduct, and Parliament plainly showed its dislike of them when invited to provide pensions for her Majesty's numerous German relatives. It was, therefore, scarcely surprising that a school of political thought should have arisen which questioned whether the monarchy was worth the cost of its maintenance.

The cry was undoubtedly strengthened by the progress of events in France, which in the year 1870 declared her third republic within a century. The leaders of the new movement were the Radical politicians Sir Charles Dilke, Charles Bradlaugh, Auberon Herbert, and Joseph Chamberlain. "The Republic must come," said the latter in a memorable utterance in 1871, "and at the rate we are moving it will come in our generation. The greater is the necessity for discussing its conditions beforehand, and for a

K

clear recognition of what we may lose as well as what we may gain."

Criticism of the royal conduct and advocacy of republicanism, which form the main features of the later *Beeton's Christmas Annuals*, had received vigorous encouragement from a sensational pamphlet of anonymous authorship which appeared in 1871, entitled *What Does She Do With It?* This pamphlet examined the royal balance-sheet in meticulous detail, arguing that the annual sum provided for the Queen by the Civil List had not been applied for the purposes for which it was expressly given, "that of maintaining for the Queen a Royal Court, and a Royal Establishment on the same scale as that of William IV." Meanwhile in the country Bradlaugh stigmatized "princely paupers," while Dilke extolled the success of a republic in a widely publicized speech to his constituents in Newcastle.

A hint of what might come was given by Beeton in the *Annual* for 1871 in an amusing skit on the siege of Paris and the rising power of the Commons entitled "The Rise of the British Republic." It was also the first sign of the alteration in the tone and style of the *Christmas Annuals*. "This country in the meanwhile," we read,

> had lost the august lady whose exalted virtue had won for her the title of Victoria the Good, and in her successor, Edward VII, the confidence of the people was apparently reposed for some time after his enthronement. It was, however, not difficult to foresee that monarchy, as an institution, was going so rapidly out of favour that, amicable and tractable as this prince was, his lease of the supreme authority would not be of long duration.

The following stanzas from *Jon Duan*, the title of the

Annual for 1874, may be taken as typical of that section
of public opinion represented by the authors:

> We sing our Court—select, sedate, demure,
>   Bound in the virtuous chains Victoria forges;
> So good, so dull, so proper, and so pure,
>   And O! so different from her Uncle George's—
> That "first of gentlemen," who, it seems sure,
>   Was fond of "life" and bacchanalian orgies;
> That blood relation of "our kings to be,"
> Who did not spell his "quean" with double "e."
> We know, we say, how very pure our Queen is,
>   And what a manager! and what a mother!
> But, though all this so very plainly seen is,
>   We cannot quite our discontentment smother.
> Her virtues we admire—but what we mean is,
>   Of two moves she should choose the one or t'other—
> The one is—Coming out amongst the nation;
> The other—Going in for Abdication.

Criticism did not stop at the shortcomings of the Queen.
It extended to the other members of the royal family,
particularly the Prince of Wales, some of whose companions and habits in private life were not considered the
most fitting preparation for the heritage of kingship.
There was much gossip about the Prince, his gambling,
racing, fondness for female society, and parties at Marlborough House. He was attacked in the Press, and even
hissed at a visit to the races.

The authors of *The Coming K——* and the other *Annuals*
made much of these failings, but in a spirit of cheerful
badinage. They really blamed the Queen for not admitting
the heir to the throne to the duties of government.

II

The titles of the last four *Beeton's Christmas Annuals* were, with their respective dates of publication, *The Coming K——* (1872), *The Siliad* (1873), *Jon Duan* (1874), and *Edward VII* (1876). They were in the main the work of S. O. Beeton, Evelyn Jerrold, and A. A. Dowty, but Beeton was always the guiding and deciding spirit in their production. Owing to the editor's absence abroad through illness for the greater part of 1875, no *Annual* appeared for that year.

The first of the series, *The Coming K——*, was chiefly concerned with the activities of the Prince of Wales and his courtiers. As we have seen, it was written in the style of the *Idylls of the King*, and was in a certain measure a parody of the Poet Laureate's popular composition.

In the so-called "idle lays" which constituted *The Coming K——* the authors cheerfully castigated the amusements of "Prince Guelpho" and his "Knights." A glaring example was the cruel sport of pigeon-shooting, which was much in fashion in the London of the sixties.

The last lay described imaginatively how the Prince's favourite horse, on whom he had placed great hopes, lost a big race at Epsom, owing to one of his enemies having given the animal a bucket of Epsom Salts. The lay ends hopefully:

And Guelpho took his "special" back to town.
And from that night became an altered man.
Henceforward did he lead a different life,
His follies all forsook, and was a King—
Take him all round, as things in this age go,
We may not have so good an one again.

In the following *Annual*, which was entitled *The Siliad, or the Siege of the Seats*, the authors returned to the fray. The piece was a mock Homeric epic written in the rhyming hexameters of Pope's translation of *The Iliad*. Its principal theme was the troubles which befell Gladstone in 1875, the last year of his Ministry; but the doings of the royal family and the manifold social evils of London occupied attention as before.

The legal difficulties in which the Prime Minister found himself in connexion with judicial and ecclesiastical patronage invoked a denunciation of the whole tribe of lawyers, with whom S. O. Beeton himself had recently already had some unpleasant dealings:

> Does not their influence English honour burke?
> Their legal mists wrap truth in endless murk?
> Since the first lawyer tempted mother Eve,
> Has not their mission been to dupe, deceive;
> To bind us in their meshes past escape,
> To tie us with interminable red tape;
> Our home to harass and our house invade?
> Who can elude the juggles of their trade?
> Who can their senseless jargon comprehend,
> Or say when their dark sway shall have an end?
> Soon one must get, if still their grasping grows,
> A parchment deed before one blows one's nose.
>
> Hear that pale man, with wasted form, wan face,
> Harangue his fellows in the market-place.
> "But shall it grow? Will not some man arise
> To sweep these legal cobwebs from our eyes;
> This age of lawyers' despotism end,
> And make a clear, plain code our guide and friend?
> So let us hope, and let this be our text—
> Down with the priests, and with the lawyers next!"

One of the topics which aroused S. O. Beeton to righteous indignation was the fate of the unmarried mother, which was far harder in the seventies than to-day. Here is a typical passage:

> A country cottage set about with trees,
> Hemmed in with flowers, and lulled with hum of bees.
> A village maiden, silly, thoughtless, wild,
> And beautiful—a petted, only child;
> A heartless villain compassing her fall;
> Seduction, ruin—there—you have it all.
> He basely lied—such scoundrels ever do—
> She loved him, fled with him, and thought him true.
> Sick of his toy, and wearying of her love,
> He threw her from him like a worn-out glove.
> And she, whate'er she does, where'er she turns,
> The bitter, shameful lesson learns,
> That, if a poor weak maiden love too well,
> She's cast forthwith into a social hell.

The third of the series, *Jon Duan*, was the one which Ward, Lock refused to publish as the *Christmas Annual* for 1874, and which was brought out by S. O. Beeton himself under the nominal imprint of another publisher. Ward, Lock's motives in declining to accept it are not altogether clear, but they were probably due to fear of being held responsible for the severe castigation of some of those in high places which the work contained. As may easily be guessed, it was modelled on Byron's *Don Juan*, and, like that production, it was not afraid to attack those whom it considered the political and social enemies of the people.

The doings and characters of the Court again occupy attention. Two of the stanzas on the Queen have already been quoted. Towards the Prince of Wales the authors continued friendly, but for his late father and his brother the Duke of Edinburgh they bore no love. The latter's bride, the Grand Duchess Marie of Russia, daughter of the Tsar Alexander II, they particularly disliked on account of her conduct in quarrelling with the popular Princess of Wales about precedence:

> Our coming Monarch's Consort's loved most dearly,
>   Loyal respect for her is most emphatic;
> And whosoever her attacks, is clearly
>   By no means well-advised or diplomatic;
> We'll trust that Marie knew no better, merely
>   Having been bred in Russ ways autocratic.
> Yet, for the future, if she'd keep her place,
> She mustn't show the Tartar, but learn grace.

The mythical hero of the poem, Jon Duan, does an instructive tour of the country, in the course of which the seamier side of London's life and society engages his attention, the ladies of Mayfair and Belgravia coming in for a severe slating:

> The wicked Demi Monde!—well, is your *monde*
>   So whole and sound and healthy? Are your wives
> Much better than "the others," and less fond
>   Of princes, lions, lead they purer lives?
> And is the Social Evil far beyond
>   Your pinchbeck imitation? If it thrives,
> Is it because it's honester and franker,
> And don't put so much cold cream on the canker?

Jon Duan concluded his tour by visiting Scotland:

> O, Land of Whiskey, Oatmeal, Bastards, Bibles;
>   O Land of Kirks, Kilts, Claymores, Kail and Cant,—
> Of lofty mountains and of very high hills,
>   Of dreary "Sawbaths," and of patriot rent;

O Land which Dr Johnson foully libels,
    To sound thy praises does our hero pant;
And to relate how, from engagements freed,
He calmly vegetated north of Tweed.

The Edinburgh "Sawbath" bored him, though,
    'Twas like being in a city of the dead;
With solemn steps, and faces full of woe,
    The people to their kirks and chapels sped,
Heard damning doctrines, droned some psalms, and so
    Went home again with Puritanic tread;
Pulled down their blinds, and in the evening glooms,
Got very drunk in their back sitting-rooms.

III

Jon Duan was the most extremely Radical of the *Christmas Annuals* which had yet appeared. W. H. Smith and Son refused to have the volume on their bookstall although they had ordered over a thousand copies in advance. It must be said in their favour, however, that their action was dictated by a threat of libel proceedings on the part of an influential financier who imagined himself defamed in the work, and they did offer to pay for the number of copies they had ordered. But Beeton would not hear of this, for the fact that they did not supply *Jon Duan* to their customers was placarded in an advertisement on all the railway bookstalls, and undoubtedly sent up the sales of the annual enormously. Within three weeks of publication 250,000 copies had been sold, and the publisher announced at the same time that the printers were "not capable of satisfying the demand for it."

The *Annual* was, of course, bitterly denounced by the Tory Press. On the other hand, its contents were justified with equal heat in all the leading Radical journals, and its popularity was easily proved by its wide circulation. If we except *Uncle Tom* and the *Household Management, Jon Duan* was probably the most successful of the Beeton publications, at any rate financially.

The last of the series was, however, in some respects the cleverest and most original. Its full title was *Edward VII. A Play on the Past and Present Times with a View to the Future.* As usual, it was projected by S. O. Beeton, but owing to his illness it appears to have been largely executed by Dowty and Jerrold. It was written in Shakespearian blank verse of the style of *Henry IV* and *Henry V*, and several notabilities of the day were thinly disguised beneath the names of characters in those plays. This latter idea was evidently Jerrold's, for we find him writing to Beeton in May 1876: "I will commence the Shakespearian scenes directly. Might not Quoins, Bardolph, and Falstaff be reinstated and modernized in connexion with our own gay Harry—Albert Edward?" The work was announced as illustrated by a treble-page frontispiece "presenting the portraits of the authors of *The Coming K——*." Here was material for another good jest, for when it was examined the illustration in question was found to represent Queen Victoria and the Prince Consort at different periods of their lives. Several reputable journals were taken in by the advance announcements, as, no doubt, the authors intended that they should be. "Did you see the attack in *The Hornet*," wrote Jerrold shortly after the *Annual* appeared, "and the magnificent leader in *The Morning Advertiser* of a week ago about the sublime impertinence

of the authors of *The Coming K——* announcing their
portraits? Bate Richards[1] will be rather sold when he
discovers he has been abusing the effigies of royalty."

The prologue to *Edward VII* was a severe piece of verse
inspired by the collision which took place between the
royal yacht *Alberta* and the schooner *Mistletoe* during the
previous summer in the Solent. As a result of the collision
the mate and two passengers on the *Mistletoe* lost their
lives. The *Alberta* was commanded by the Prince of
Leiningen, and the Queen was on board at the time. The
popular impression was that the captain had been guilty
of negligence, but the verdict of the coroner's jury was
that the collision was accidental, though a rider was added
to the effect that the navigating officer of the royal yacht
had committed an error of judgment, and they recommended a slower speed on the part of the *Alberta* during
the yachting season and that a more efficient look-out be
kept. Public feeling was considerably roused by the
incident, and the matter raised in Parliament, where
Disraeli, the Prime Minister, had considerable difficulty in
smoothing it over. It was therefore a fitting subject for
the notice of the authors of *The Coming K——* in their
new annual. Two verses from the prologue are given
below.

> *Off the Isle of Wight. Lat. Too Great. Lon. Doubtful.*
> *Page of a book not written up by the Quartermaster*
> *or Captain of the "Alberta" on August 18th, 1875.*

The Mistletoe sailed in the Solent Sea,
Scarce three knots an hour went she;
And her passengers all were blithe and gay,
Keeping their summer holiday.

[1] Editor of the *Morning Advertiser*.

None thought of danger—the sea was calm,
Not even the ladies felt a qualm;
For trim was the yacht and brave the crew,
And at the helm was the Captain true.
Oh! the Mistletoe bow!

Upon her track a steamer bore down,
And her freight was the wearer of England's crown.
She was mann'd by a crew of pick'd seamen,
And the most Serene Prince Leiningen.
Away she tore at a slashing rate,
For woe! if the train two seconds should wait;
And woe to the yacht that dared to stay
When the Queen of England passed that way.
Oh! the Mistletoe bow!

Edward VII may be described as a Shakespearian parody in seven acts. The scenes were laid in such diverse places as "Albor Castle" (Windsor Castle), "Malbarrow House" (Marlborough House), "Cap and Bells, Westcheap" (Gaiety Restaurant, Strand), "The Coal Scoop Company's Hall," the Suez Canal, and India. The principal living characters were "Queen Victa" (Queen Victoria), "Prince Guelpho" (Edward, Prince of Wales), "Prince Humpburgh" (Alfred, Duke of Edinburgh), "Prince Bragthaw" (Arthur, Duke of Connaught), "Prince Phleopold" (Prince Leopold), "Kamdux" (George, Duke of Cambridge), "Lord Hope Forlorn" (the Marquess of Lorne), "Quoins" (Francis Knollys, Private Secretary to the Prince of Wales), "Falstaff" (Lord Henry Paget, Chief Equerry to the Prince of Wales), "Dr Redlion" (W. H. Russell, the well-known *Times* war correspondent), "Sweteburn" (Algernon Charles Swinburne), "Scala" (George Augustus Sala), and "Toipay Konnore" (T. P. O'Connor), at that time a penurious journalist at the beginning of his career.

The greater part of the play was devoted to the castigation of "the vices and follies of the age," as in the previous annuals, but the last two acts constituted an amazing forecast of "things to come." Great Britain is dragged into the Eastern conflagration which had been brewing between Russia and Turkey, she declares war on the Tsar, the Prince of Wales leads the Army in person against the enemy, and after the issue has been decided victoriously and the Russian Army routed it is announced that Queen Victoria has abdicated, and the Prince of Wales ascends the throne as "Edward VII."

In the final scene the new monarch addresses his victorious troops:

> Full worthy of my now exalted post
> 'Tis not within man's means to wholly be;
> But, soldiers, I will try to bear myself
> Like a good Englishman: give me your aid,
> And with my Queen beside me, I will seek
> England's first place among the powers to keep.

IV

The Republican wave of the seventies gained considerable support in the more Radical parts of the country, but it is doubtful whether the monarchy had at any time very much to fear from it. It soon spent itself, and before even the appearance of the last of *Beeton's Christmas Annuals* it could safely be counted as a thing of the past. The bubble had in reality been pricked as early as 1872. In that year the Prince of Wales recovered from a serious attack of typhoid fever, and the occasion was treated as one of national thanksgiving by a service in St Paul's Cathedral.

Two days later an attempt was made to assassinate the Queen as she was driving through the Park, and this incident accelerated the revival of royal popularity. Disraeli's success in persuading her Majesty to appear in public more frequently, and even to open Parliament in person for two years in succession, completed the process. The mass of the people disliked the Republican idea as a product of Jacobin France, much in the same way as they distrust the political theories of Communist Russia to-day.

But even if Beeton and his literary associates tilted in vain at the Republican windmill, their charges were effective in other directions. What the Queen described in a celebrated letter to the editor of *The Times* as "the *immense* danger and evil of the wretched frivolity and levity of the views and lives of the Higher Classes," as well as other grave social abuses, were thoroughly exposed in the last four *Christmas Annuals*. Beeton's attempts to 'clean up' some of the more scandalous features in the life of the nation, whose existence many people were too hypocritical to admit, were well judged; and though their author was destined to pass away before his time, his name still lives in his works, and is remembered with gratitude by all who have striven in the cause of social improvements. It had already become a household word in the English language through the *Book of Household Management* which he had inspired his wife to carry out on the lines originally suggested by him.

Chapter VII

FINIS

FOR ten years after his wife's death S. O. Beeton lived on at Greenhithe, first at Mount Pleasant and later in the old Coast Guard cottage near by, sharing the establishment with the Brownes. In the upbringing of his two boys, Orchart ("Dorch") and Mayson ("Dace") the mother's place was largely taken by Mrs Browne, a woman of strong maternal instincts, who was still editing, under his literary control, if no longer under his ownership, *The Englishwoman's Domestic Magazine* and *The Young Englishwoman*. On their side the boys regarded her as their mother and called her "Mamma." Indeed, she did everything for them that a mother would normally do, such as looking after their clothes and getting them ready for school. "She was a very good mother to me," remarked Mayson after he had grown up. He remembered how she made a greatcoat for him out of his father's "chequered peg top trousers, complete with velvet cuffs and roll collar."

In due course the two boys were sent to a private school at Exmouth, kept by an old Oxford rowing Blue, the Rev. C. R. Carr, who, as Mayson subsequently remembered, "knew well how to wield his cane."

The following letters written to the boys by their father during the summer term of 1874 show how fond he was of his young sons, and how, in spite of increasing ill-health and business worries, he studied their interests.

GREENHITHE,
April 28 '74

MY DEAR BOYS,

I had your letters this afternoon, and I have sent them to Paris with my letter to Mamma; she will be home, I expect, by Saturday or Sunday. Mr Gard,[1] Mr Tyler,[2] and Mr Leaker were here yesterday, but I am alone today. Little Puss has had four kittens—two have been drowned; the others are beautifully marked, looking something like the lizard wh. by the bye Tommy caught and killed on the terrace. Your thrush sits closely to her nest, and does not move when I go to look at her. I have found outside the gate in the road opposite Breakneck Hill a tribe of Mason Bees, (not Mayson Beetons); they have hundreds of little holes into wh. they are constantly carrying their honey, pollen etc. Rough[3] is very funny, he cannot understand puss always keeping in the basket with her young ones; when you come home, the kittens will be playing about, I have no doubt.

You are very lucky in your cricket matches; bathing won't begin, I suppose, till May. We have strong winds here today, but the weather is very fine; we want some rain, however, and the roads are very dusty. Poor Barrow, fifth! I am sorry to hear he is getting, as you say, worse and worse. Have you had any games at Chess?—it is hardly the weather for that however, as it is better to be playing out of doors. Has Dace read the Waterm'tch and The Two Admirals? I can send him some more books to read, if he wishes. I hope he is keeping out of impots and

---

[1] A very old friend, who had "roughed it up country" in the Australian bush in the early days of its settlement, and who returned to England to devise a patent for making "plate cloths"—*i.e.*, rough cotton cloths soaked in plate powder used for cleaning silver, so as to make one operation, instead of requiring the application of two cloths.

[2] Charles Tyler, formerly a partner in Ward, Lock, and Co., and a close friend of Beeton's.

[3] The family terrier.

punishments; and if he can get to be Number Two instead of Three, and have a good character from Mr Carr it will delight me and all of us very much.

My love to both of you, my dear boys—

Your loving Father.

GREENHITHE,
July 9th, '74

MY DEAR DORCH,

Your letter of last Sunday was duly received, and I was delighted to read that you are not afraid of stopping a ball, and that you have a good eye for a good "throw in." Go in for bowling, as much as you can; it is splendid exercise, and makes a man very patient and persevering.

You were first in the last examn.—that is good news. Who are your competitors, and who was the boy who had 62 marks to your 49? You have evidently a tough job, and will have to work hard to come out first. I hope you will, with all my heart, but if you can't be first, come out as near the top as possible. English is your weak point, because you do not read books enough; and I do sincerely wish you may get a greater taste for seeing what all the greatest men in the world have said and written.

The weather during the last few days has been tropical, that is to say, the heat has been such as is felt in the tropics; —there is almost always a fresh breeze, here; but in London, where I was yesterday, the heat was fearful. So, I suppose it is with you. Don't get too hot, and don't lie about when you are too hot, nor keep in a draught, which is the worst of all. I don't know whether Mamma told you that we have now a Beehive with its inhabitants, in the garden— close to your gardens. Your crops are growing well, and I have had several fine strawberries from the plants near yours. Gooseberries, cherries, as well as strawberries we have plenty of; and there are plenty of apples and pears coming on. I'm afraid you will be a little late for the gooseberries; still, I hope some will be left. Gerty[1] in her loose box in the poultry yard enjoys herself very much; we let her into the field to eat the grass, and she is as gentle as a lamb. Old Moreau[2] gets quieter every day; and Rough, noisier; he barks at every one of us as we come in, but doesn't take notice of strangers—he is a curious old fellow. His mother has had another litter, and one of the pups, less than half Rough's size, is exactly like him. Goodbye. Dace did not write last Sunday; give him a hint to do it, when you write: God bless you.

Your affectionate Father.

GREENHITHE,
July 17th, 1874

MY DEAR DORCH,

Dace writes me that he has no postage stamps: let him have some of those sent you, if he asks for one, as you have had plenty for all the letters written.

I am very glad to see you were put on to bowl; it is very grand to bat and knock the ball about, but he who can get out his opponents by bowling, or catching, or "throwing in" well, is of more use to his side even than a great batsman. They play a good deal now in the park, and I trust we shall be able to get some play somewhere when you come home.

In a few days I suppose we shall have your holiday letters; and we shall be delighted to see your brown faces once more. I have been better lately, and I hope to be able to be more with you out of doors than before. Most of the

---

[1] His mare.

[2] A big French mule, whom Goubaud had sent to England to save his life when the siege of Paris was imminent in 1871.

L

larger yachts have gone to the Westward from the Thames, that is, to the Isle of Wight and the South Coast, where they begin to race now. We have still, here, quite a little fleet. Have you seen the Comet? It is a wonderful sight seen thro' a large telescope; I do not know if there is one at your school.

Marlborough, I see, has won the Public Schools Prize in rifle shooting at Wimbledon; it is the first time that school has carried it off.

I hope you will work up your Arithmetic, as when once you have conquered the difficulties of the first steps, Mathematics are exceedingly interesting.

Mr Gard has been here the last two evenings; he sends his kind love to you both. We have plenty of apples and pears on our little trees, wh. are growing nicely. Rough is all right in health, but is a nuisance, for he barks too much; he has a little brother, from another litter, wh. Gibson showed me—exactly like Ruff, about one third of his weight: it is quite funny to see him, he walks and moves so exactly like Rough (or Ruff).

I wish you both success in your exams., and with best love am,

Yours ever affectionately,
Father.

LONDON, 13 FURNIVAL'S INN,
Friday Morning,
July 24th, '74

MY DEAR BOYS,

Your holiday letters came duly to hand at Greenhithe—also your letters upon your cricket, bathing, sports, etc. How did you get on in the 100 yards Bathing Race, or Swimming Match rather? I have been in London for a

few days, so as to do some work without having to come
up to London every day.

I am going to-morrow to Dunstable (Bedfordshire) to
see Mr Gard[1] and shall probably return here on Monday
and stay till Thursday, when I will go down with you,
after meeting you at Waterloo.

I hope to see you well and happy, and with all affection,
am,

Your loving Father.

P.S. I enclose cheque for £2 (for Mr Carr) wh. will
pay yr. journey, 2nd class, as usual; and give you a few
shillings for extras.

II

Early in 1875 Beeton left England for Italy, accompanied
by his friend and literary colleague A. A. Dowty. The
first part of the journey was made by rail, apparently to
Marseilles, and thence by sea to Naples. "Here at last,"
he wrote from Naples towards the end of February,

after a six hundred miles railway tearing to pieces and a
steam boat shaking of about the same distance. Worth all
the cost and trouble twenty times over. . . . But it is
diabolically cold, the east wind coming round corners at
you, more fiercely even than in England, I think. . . . I'm
getting over the fatigue of my travel, and I shall do well
I'm persuaded; but can't get over the feeling that I'm
shirking the hardships of life too much. I'm a bit of a
Puritan in this respect, and I'm not fond of myself unless
I've got a crux or two on my shoulders.

The last sentence was eminently characteristic of the
man. He was happiest when he had a heavy cross to bear.

[1] The chalk cliffs near Dunstable supplied him with the powder for his "plate
cloths."

And he was to have one, even in Naples. His companion Dowty was taken ill, and Beeton, though far from fit himself, insisted on nursing him through the crisis and convalescence. The result was that when he returned to England in the autumn the state of his own health was considerably worse than when he set out on his Continental journey.

Nevertheless, in spite of the physical handicap and the periods of intense suffering which he underwent, Beeton determined to start up afresh as a publisher, now that he was released from the employment of Ward and Lock. To this end he took offices at 39 and 40 Bedford Street, Covent Garden, and arranged with his friend Weldon, who was conducting a small publishing business on his own, to act as his publisher for the books and magazines which he was contemplating. But he had not reckoned with his old employers. Fresh injunctions were threatened if he proceeded to bring out works under his own imprint. On the other hand, Beeton's case against Ward and Lock was that they were making what he considered to be an improper use of his name by publishing works with his name attached to them, "of the nature and qualities of which he never had the means of judging," as by the agreement with Ward and Lock he alleged the right to have had; and that "others of the publications contained views and opinions of which he disapproved and which he contended were, or might be, injurious to his character." He therefore decided to seek the ruling of the Court of Chancery without delay. The publication selected as a test was a work entitled *Beeton's Book of Universal Etiquette*, in whose production Beeton had taken no part whatever.

The Vice-Chancellor, Sir Richard Malins, was again on

the Bench. Curiously enough, he delivered judgment on December 21, 1875, exactly a year to the day on which he had ruled in the previous action. He was with Beeton on the principle of the case, but against him on the point of time, holding that so far as the publications specifically complained of went, he had come too late for the assistance of the court. The fact that Beeton had been abroad for reasons of health for the greater part of a year was unfortunately no excuse. He went on to say that if the cause were now being heard on its merits he should hold that on such a contract as that which existed here one publisher had no right to use the name of another as attached to works with which that other had nothing to do. The plaintiff had received his salary for services for the past year, and for the use of his name for several of the defendant's publications.

"Both the plaintiff and his late wife had acquired a high reputation in connexion with works for which the demand was great, and the use therefore of the plaintiff's name was of considerable value to the defendants." Now, Ward and Lock said that they had an unlimited right under the agreement to use the plaintiff's name in connexion with works in which he was not concerned. There was, however, a difference between "future" publications and the Christmas annual "Beeton's Christmas Annual." With respect to that, he had decided a year ago that, as Ward and Lock had purchased the copyright of and the right to use the plaintiff's name in the publication of it, and as he had agreed to give his whole time to their service and not to engage in any other business, he must be restrained from advertising a rival work. But the judge went on to say that in his opinion the plaintiff had the right to know and to see things published under his own name which might damage his reputation. He had the right to see that the use of his name was a proper one. This contract was determinable on a specified notice by either party, and if the plantiff gave the requisite notice he would be entitled to stop the subsequent publication by the defendants of any work with his name to it.

So far, that only regarded the individual parties to the agreement; but as to the public generally, it was manifestly unfair to publish the work with the name of an author attached to it who had nothing to do with it. Whatever deceived the public was a fraud upon it, and if anyone bought a book purporting, on the face of it, to be the work of a particular author, when it was not really his, such a purchaser would be deceived. The plaintiff here swore in his evidence that he never would have authorised the publication of many of the things published under his name by the defendants and which he had not revised. He swore too that many of the things published would damage his reputation. If he proved all that at the hearing he would have a right to restrain the publications. But the present was only an interlocutory application; and with reference to the book on "Etiquette" it was advertised as long ago as April, 1875. The plantiff said he did not know of the advertisement in the catalogue for he was ill and travelling abroad for his health; but having regard to the plaintiff's connection with the defendant's business, it must be presumed that he did, as he was bound to know what they were doing, and there was on that ground no excuse whatever for his not having come to their court sooner than the end of November last. Moreover, the defendants had incurred considerable expense in the preparation of these works.

Although, therefore, the judge was in favour of the plaintiff's case so far as the principle of it was concerned, he said that he felt bound to rule that Beeton had come for his interlocutory injunction at too late a moment. So strong, however, was the judge's opinion on the principle of the case that he could but suggest to both sides —"where, as in most of these instances, each was partly right and partly wrong"—an arrangement of some sort; or, if that was impossible, that the defendants should not proceed to the publication of any works to which the plaintiff's name was attached without his sanction.

It only remains to add that Ward and Lock took the judge's hint, and thenceforward confined their use of Beeton's name to new editions of old publications like the *Book of Household Management* and the *Christmas Annual*.

III

As he was abroad for the greater part of 1875, S. O. Beeton was unable to plan an annual to follow up the success created by *Jon Duan*. Just before setting out for Italy, however, he contrived to assist materially at the launching of a new magazine, edited by his friend Mrs Browne, who had also severed her connexion with Ward and Lock. This was called *Myra's Journal of Dress and Fashion*, "Myra" having been her pen-name when she was editress of *The Young Englishwoman*, and it was the first journal to appear in this country exclusively devoted to the two chief interests of women. Beeton went into such questions as costs and 'lay-out' with great care, and its initial success was due in large measure to his help.

"What is wanted," he remarked to Weldon, who, he had arranged, should be the publisher, "is a large constituency, first of all, so that you may have large numbers of people to appeal to instead of the restricted few whom Ward and Lock have managed to come down to with *The Young Englishwoman* and *The Englishwoman's Domestic Magazine*." Full-sized diagrams for "cutting out" all kinds of dresses, including children's, were issued, together with paper patterns, or "models." The latest information from the "Grand Magasin du Louvre" in Paris was given, while the house of Goubaud continued to supply its well-known coloured fashion plates. In fact, all the novelties devised by Beeton in his early publications were employed, with such improvements as their author suggested. Beeton returned from Naples to find *Myra's Journal of Dress and Fashion* fairly launched and selling well under Mrs Browne's able editorship, as it continued to do for many years after his death.

And now to turn to another aspect of Beeton's publishing work at this period. Among those who called on Beeton at his new offices in Bedford Street was a young Irishman named T. P. O'Connor, still in his twenties. They were introduced to each other by Evelyn Jerrold. At this time the future founder and editor of *The Star*, the doyen of Fleet Street and the Father of the House of Commons, was a struggling and penurious journalist, more often than not unemployed and in want of a meal. They at once became friends, and T. P. O'Connor would listen more or less spellbound as the older man talked, noting how every hour or so a glass of medicine or cup of soup was brought to him to drink. In his autobiography the Irishman has left a vivid picture of the invalid publisher, whose helpful suggestions gave him his first real start in life and first brought him public notice:

A strange, interesting, attractive man S. O. Beeton was; I have reason to remember him gratefully, for he was very kind to me on the whole, and very considerate. I met him in the period of his decline; for he had lost his wife, who had been so great a helpmate to him; had left a firm of publishers, Ward, Lock and Tyler; had not quite set up for himself; and, above all, had permanently and irretrievably lost his health. He was almost a startling sight when first you met him. I have never seen so thin a man who yet was able to live. Indeed when first you saw him, you were only conscious of a pair of eyes—large, brilliant, burning, a beautiful and almost dazzling blue-grey in colour—they seemed to be the only living thing in the man to have alone survived the wreck of the rest of the frame. A ramrod with two shining little lamps near the top—that is something like what S. O. Beeton was in the days when I made his acquaintance.

In some respects he might have stood for Don Quixote; for, in addition to this phenomenal thinness, he wore his beard in a peculiar style. It was a beautiful grey, like the eyes—and it was brought down to a point just as is the typical beard of the Spaniard. The intellect and the spirit of the man, however, shone as brightly as the eyes. He was a ferocious Radical; was a brilliant and fervent conversationalist; and often would talk to me for long hours together to the detriment of his health sometimes, and to the great alarm of those who were watching over the flickering candle of his existence.

The object of young O'Connor's first visit to Bedford Street was to apply for work as a publisher's reader. He had just been to see a member of the publishing house of

Cassell on the same errand, and had been advised instead to try his hand at writing books. Such advice he was inclined to regard as a bitter joke, for, in his own words,

> writing books seemed to me then so terrible, gigantic, hopeless, an enterprise that it would have been very midsummer madness and self-conceit on my part to attempt the task; and to recommend a man almost driven to despair to attempt the impossible seemed to me a wantonly additional insult to injury.

His surprise, therefore, was considerable when Beeton tendered him precisely similar advice. "I was once more aghast at the proposition," he subsequently admitted, "and was inclined to refuse it. But he talked on, and at last he suggested an idea which struck me as a very good one, and one that fell in with my own taste and pursuits."

The idea was that O'Connor should write a book describing the great scenes in the Houses of Parliament. While there had been a number of isolated accounts of such scenes, there never had been any collected and complete description of them, and Beeton suggested that the young journalist should look into the subject and see what prospects there were in it. Accordingly O'Connor went off to the Reading Room of the British Museum, the happy hunting-ground of all aspirants to literary fame, and there he set about collecting material for the projected work. One of the first scenes which he investigated was the occasion of Disraeli's maiden speech in the House of Commons, which was delivered in dramatic and unusual circumstances. He asked for the newspapers of the period.

> I remember distinctly the strange feeling of half-affrighted expectations with which I opened the papers, uncertain

whether they would contain the historic words which had
been attributed to Disraeli, or whether these were either the
blurred recollections or the legendary invention which came
long afterwards. I read paper after paper; to my delight
and surprise I found the speech reported in full and almost
in the same words in all of them. I got a friend to copy out
the entire speech while I looked into other things, and then
I brought the copy to Mr Beeton. He was as surprised and
delighted as I was, and he saw a confirmation of his idea
that a book called *Scenes in the House* would make a readable
and saleable volume.

O'Connor went back to the British Museum, and the
more he thought about this speech the more interested he
became in the career of its author. After some further
hunting among the old newspaper files he decided to
abandon the original project suggested by Beeton and
write a biography of the Tory leader. With this idea
Beeton readily agreed, and O'Connor accordingly set to
work. "I little knew when I started out on the task what a
gigantic business it was going to be," he has said;

indeed the book nearly killed me. . . . In order to write
the book I had to go through forty years of Hansard; and
Hansard for one year usually consists of five or six big
volumes. I had to read almost every line Disraeli ever
spoke, whether it was at hustings at election times or to his
constituents during the Parliamentary vacations; I had to
read all his own works which amounted to something like
a library in themselves; and, in short, I had to spend on
this work considerable industry.

The outcome of this industry was *Benjamin Disraeli,
Earl of Beaconsfield*, which, as its author said, "was bought
at a price which few now would be able or willing to pay."

It appeared in two volumes. The first, which brought the stateman's life down to the year 1846, was published by S. O. Beeton from 39 Bedford Street; and the second, which was not completed until after Beeton's death, came out under the imprint of "Goubaud and Son" from the same offices.

While this work was being written O'Connor was so absorbed that it was difficult for him to seek out any other work, with the result that, as he has confessed, his entire income consisted of the occasional cheques for £5 which Beeton gave him. He was, in fact, in considerable straits, and for part of the time he was so poor that even paper was a serious consideration to him. He has left on record how glad he was when a friend who was a chemist gave him a large bundle of leaflets setting forth the merits of some plaster or ointment. As the leaflets were printed on one side only, the poverty-stricken writer was able to use the other for his manuscript, and a large portion of the book was written in this way. It brought credit both to author and publisher, though it was on the whole un-flattering to its subject, as befitted the pen of a Liberal of the advanced school. But while it marked for T. P. O'Connor the beginning of a successful career both as journalist and M.P. in the coming struggle for Home Rule for Ireland, for S. O. Beeton it was the end of things earthly. Shortly after it had been issued the flickering candle of his existence was extinguished.

IV

To conclude with the story of the last few months, Beeton, on his return from Italy, gave up his house at

Greenhithe, and went to live in rooms over the new offices which he had taken at 39 Bedford Street. To have built up a business afresh in the noisy neighbourhood of Covent Garden while living there as well would have severely taxed the physical powers of a strong man, but to one whose health was all but completely shattered the effort could only prove fatal. Nevertheless he carried on his work cheerfully with the knowledge that there was little chance of escape now from the toils of disease. Trials and tribulations he passed over lightly and bore with Spartan courage; even the defalcation of his principal assistant, whom he had long trusted, though it caused him grief as well as financial loss, did not make him despair.

Towards the end of the Christmas term, in 1876, he wrote the following letter to his youngest son, still at school in Exmouth:

39 BEDFORD STREET
13 Nov. '76

MY DEAR DACE,

I have been expecting to see your hand-write, as they say in Scotland, for many days. Mamma has written you and sent you things since her return; and I wrote you both in one letter just before we left. Let me know how you are, and what's the last new thing. I have just read a new book, intending to publish it next year for boys, "Captain Kyd, The Wizard of the Sea"—a wonderful catalogue of adventures. Ask me for it when you come home, with some others written by the same author, Ingraham.

As it is now almost certain that you will spend your holidays in London, we are going to do the best we can to make you enjoy them:—we must go in for another and bigger Branpie; and Charly Tyler has just been in and promises that two at least of his "young ladies" shall come to the B.P.

The canary that Mamma bought for Miss Beale died of the "pip," whilst we were away in Paris—he was getting a beautiful bird; and I miss him very much. Mamma tells me that those little red-wax billed birds of hers are beginning to sing, and sound like a little musical box. I must ask Aunt Carrie to buy another canary at the old Portsmo' bird shop as Philip is coming to London shortly, I believe. (He couldn't come along—could he?)

What's the game afoot now? Here, to-day, it is so dark that candles and gas are alight everywhere in all the rooms —not like sunshiny Italy, nor, I hope, like Exmouth. A few weeks now and you will be travelling towards the East, I hope. The last news, by the bye, from the East, is a piece of cheek from the Czar in answer to a first piece by my Lord Beaconsfield.

You will write me a few lines, between your meals and yr. mathematics, I hope.

Your loving Father,
with his kindest affection.

When the boys came home for the holidays *Edward VII* was just out, the last of the *Christmas Annuals* which S. O. Beeton personally supervised. Its immediate success seemed to stimulate the sick publisher with fresh spirits and energy. He lived his own schooldays again, as he took his two schoolboy sons to the pantomime and shared their branpie. But it was the final bright flame thrown up by the dying fire. When the boys came home again at Easter he was too ill to take them out; for he now lay in bed or on a sofa all day, propped up by pillows, pale and gaunt, with hollow cheeks and the pallor of death on his face.

Dr Mackenzie, the doctor who attended him, was already

well known in London; a decade later his name was to become the subject of the most bitter international controversy by reason of his treatment of a royal patient. At the time of Beeton's illness Morell Mackenzie was barely forty years of age, and he had not met the Crown Prince of Germany. He was still conducting a general practice, although he was also the leading throat specialist in the country. He had a wide circle of acquaintances, particularly in theatrical and literary circles, and he had the reputation of being a generous host as well as an entertaining talker. He visited Beeton almost daily, and the two men became firm and affectionate friends.

Soon after the two boys returned to school for the summer term Mackenzie had their father moved to a sanatorium outside London, at Richmond, Sudbrook Park, in a final effort to prolong his life. Here the patient fought his last battle, short and sharp. Then when the flowers which he loved so well were in full blossom and all nature seemed joyous he lay still and at peace. The end came on June 6, 1877. He was buried beside Isabella in Norwood Cemetery, where a white marble headstone, later erected by their son Mayson, commemorates their unique partnership.

Many generous and warm-hearted tributes were paid to Sam Beeton's memory. Among the most sincere was the obituary notice which his friend Dowty prepared for the *London Figaro*. "How energetic and how full of enterprise and spirits he was," wrote Dowty,

in spite of his ever present foe, those only who knew him well can appreciate. To the last his vitality was most extraordinary and his strength of mind never for a moment failed him, even when the fell disease was at its worst. . . .

He was courageous well nigh to temerity, and possessed the subtle power of inspiring all who worked with him with the most sanguine hopes of success; a power that is only given to the few, and is so largely developed in those who become leaders of men. . . . An ardent lover of nature and a firm believer in the goodness of the Creator, Mr Beeton hated with an intense abhorrence anything that smacked of bigotry or sectarian prejudice. In politics he held advanced views, being almost Quixotic in his well-meant efforts to do the masses good. . . . As a friend Mr Beeton was most constant and devoted, whilst those who have been unfortunate enough to be in a position antagonistic to him must admit the chivalrous nature of his opposition, even whilst suffering from its thoroughness and success. . . . His funeral was a private one, but the few near friends who gathered round his grave could not but be sad when they thought what a real man, what a true and genial friend, what a fond father, and what a noble and gentle soul had been taken from their midst.

For the following Christmas Dowty and Jerrold brought out an annual entitled *Finis*, and announced it as "published for the benefit of the children of the late S. O. Beeton." It included his portrait and the following verses *in memoriam*:

> His nature chivalrous recoiled
> From dirty work; he could not see
> And not denounce, rank roguery—
> The crafty villain oft he foiled.

> Of deeply reverent soul possess'd,
> In Nature, Nature's God he found,
> His Godhead manifest around,
> No stone could he of God divest.

The upbringing of the two orphan children was completed by the Brownes, who had shared the house at Greenhithe with Sam Beeton. Charly Browne worked in the Westminster Fire Office, a few doors away from Sam's last publishing headquarters in Bedford Street, while Mrs Matilda Browne, "a second mother," as Mayson later described her, carried on with her journalistic work as well as looking after the two boys during the holidays. Now that they were orphaned she did her best to take their mother's place. Indeed, as we have seen, both boys always referred to her as "Mamma."

From Mr Carr's preparatory school at Exmouth the boys were sent in due course to a public school. Marlborough was chosen. From here Orchart ("Orchy"), the elder, went into the Army, which he made his career. He lived to enjoy an honourable retirement, dying in 1947 at the age of eighty-five. Mayson ("Dace"), the younger of the two boys, went from Marlborough to Magdalen College, Oxford, where he had won a demyship, and took his degree in history. He died, after a varied and distinguished career, in the same year as his brother.[1]

IV

Such is the brief but full life-story of Samuel and Isabella Beeton. Theirs was a finely blended domestic and literary partnership, and, except for the loss of the first two children born to them, one of complete happiness while it lasted. Happily for her, Isabella Beeton was spared the pain of witnessing the suffering and misfortunes which befell her husband in his later years. He, on the other hand, to quote

[1] See Appendix and Foreword.

M

his friend Dowty, "never ceased to lament the loss of one who was not only possessed with the most complete sympathy for her husband's plans and projects, but was enabled practically and efficiently to aid him in their consummation." In his scheme of things her loss was in reality irreplaceable. No wonder he and his family dreaded the approach of the anniversaries of his marriage and her death, which when they came round each year threw him into prolonged fits of mental depression.

Samuel Beeton was a pioneer. And, in Lucy Smiles's words, he "had the fate of all pioneers—he sowed and others reaped." His ideas and projects produced immense profits, but not for him. Nearly half a century before the development of modern journalism Beeton realized that journalism of the future must appeal to women as well as men. News of fashions and the home would find as eager and more lucrative readers than the doings of Parliament and the City. Prize competitions and columns and pages exclusively devoted to feminine interests and pursuits were the principal literary novelties initiated by S. O. Beeton, and since then it is not too much to say that they have revolutionized modern journalism. Dress, kitchen, children, toilet, social gossip, are topics of prime importance to the women of the country, and no journal which caters for the general public can afford to ignore them to-day.

No critical estimate of the literary achievements of Samuel and Isabella Beeton is possible without bearing in mind that their work was mutually complementary. As we have seen, *Mrs Beeton's Book of Household Management* for half a century after its first appearance came as a most welcome wedding-gift to many thousands of young housewives, who were able, under its influence and guidance, to build up and maintain happy and comfortable homes. In founding a healthy periodical literature both for the women and for the young folk of the country generally, as well as disseminating knowledge in its printed form popularly and cheaply, and also courageously attacking the more glaring political and social abuses of the times, S. O. Beeton devoted his life to the service of a most worthy cause. Husband and wife alike gained a reward greater than any money could buy in the pleasure and benefits which their united efforts bestowed upon the public from "The Sign of the Bee-hive."

Appendix

THE LATE SIR MAYSON BEETON, K.B.E.

LIKE his father, Mayson Beeton was a pioneer, and, like him, he married young. On leaving Magdalen College, Oxford, where he gained his degree in history, he married Louisa Swinley, eldest daughter of Dr William Price Jones, of Surbiton. Mayson started his career as an independent journalist, and in collaboration with his wife produced a very attractive domestic magazine called *Hearth and Home*.

Mrs Mayson Beeton also produced an excellent cookery-book (*Myra's Cookery Book*), and family history so far tended to repeat itself. Then, after a few years, Mayson, who was a great friend of Alfred Harmsworth (afterwards Lord Northcliffe), was asked by him to go out to the West Indies as Special Correspondent for the *Daily Mail* to report on the whole question of the sugar industry there, which was at the time being studied by a Royal Commission. This was just the kind of pioneer work that appealed to him; he accepted, the enterprise was most successful, and led to his appointment as Secretary to the Anti-bounty League. For five years he took a very active part in the campaign, which resulted in the abolition of the foreign sugar bounties and the suppression of cartels by the Brussels Convention of 1902.

Just as this chapter in his life was successfully completed it so happened that the Harmsworths had another pioneer enterprise in view which he was specially fitted to undertake. This time it was to prospect for suitable territory which would give a sure supply of paper for newsprint from wood-pulp for their rapidly expanding Press. He accepted the responsibility, and as a result of his pioneering survey of forest-lands in Sweden, Canada, and Newfoundland (in Newfoundland involving the exploration of completely virgin forest), 3000 square miles of forest-land was acquired in Central Newfoundland. Grand Falls on Exploit river was included in the concession, and this provided the water-power essential for the large pulp- and paper-mills which were finally established there. The Anglo-Newfoundland Development Company was formed to carry out this great undertaking, and Mayson Beeton was its first President. He also became a Director of the *Daily Mail* Trust.

During the First World War Mayson Beeton organized and administered the Newfoundland Forestry Corps, and also worked in the Finance Department of the Ministry of Munitions. For these services to his country he was created a K.B.E. in 1920.

His hobby in later years was to collect books and prints of old London, and he accumulated a valuable library on this subject, which he subsequently presented to the nation. This interest led to the production in collaboration with the late Beresford Chancellor of a fine folio edition of that part of Defoe's *Tour thro' the Whole Island of Great Britain* which referred to London. It was published by Batsford and Co. in 1929, and ranks as a collector's work.

The Mayson Beetons had a very happy married life, clouded only by the untimely death of their only son in a motor accident when a schoolboy of sixteen. They celebrated their golden wedding in 1938.

Lady Beeton died in 1943, and Sir Mayson in 1947. They left three married daughters—Marjorie (Mrs L. G. Kilby), Audrey (Mrs G. Murray Levick), and Isabel (Mrs G. S. Farebrother). Their grandson, Rodney Levick (whose father was medical officer to Captain Scott's last Antarctic expedition), inherited all MSS. which had been preserved relating to

Mayson Beeton's own and his parents' lives, which (quoting from his will) "may be of interest to posterity as throwing interesting sidelights on the Victorian and Edwardian periods." Material from these documents has contributed with the family's permission to form the basis of this book.

Index

ACTON, ELIZA, 88

Adams, W. H. Davenport, 51, 124

Albany, Leopold, Duke of, 155

Amateur Casual, The (Greenwood), 52

America, S. O. Beeton's visit to, 43–44, 45

Archer, Thomas, 126

Asquith, Herbert Henry, Earl of Oxford and Asquith, 19 *n.*

BARONESS PUDDING, recipe for, 81

Bartholme, Anne, 21 *and n.*, 22 *n.*

Bassin d'Arcachon, 80

Bayonne, 80

Beecher, Rev. H. W., 43

Beeton, Eliza (stepsister of S. O. Beeton), 53

Beeton, Frederick P. (stepbrother of S. O. Beeton), 66 *and n.*

Beeton, Isabella, ancestry and birth of, 19–28, 58; education of, 59; becomes engaged, 59; opposition of her family, 60–64; correspondence with S. O. Beeton, 60–78; marriage of, 78; contributes to husband's publications, 81, 115; begins her *Book of Household Management*, 81, 83; birth and death of first child, 82–83, 116; birth of second son, 83; in France, 83–85; in Killarney, 85–87; success of her book, 88 *et seq.*; her method of collecting recipes, 102–104; death of second child, 112; birth of third child, 113; in Germany, 113–114; in France again, 114–115; death of, 128; her husband's tribute, 130–131

Beeton, John (great-grandfather of S. O. Beeton), 15–16

Beeton, Mrs John, 15

Beeton, Sir Mayson ("Dace," son of S. O. Beeton), 129, 158–163, 173–174, 175, 177

Beeton, Orchart ("Dorch," son of S. O. Beeton), 113, 127, 129, 158–163, 174, 175, 177

Beeton, Samuel (grandfather of S. O. Beeton), 15–18, 29

Beeton, Samuel Orchart, ancestry and birth of, 15–18; education of, 29–30; becomes partner in Charles H. Clarke and Co., 30; and the publication of *Uncle Tom's Cabin*, 33 *et seq.*; visits America, 41–44, 45; inaugurates *The Englishwoman's Domestic Magazine*, 45–49; inaugurates *The Boy's Own Magazine*, 50–54; parts company with Clarke, 57; becomes engaged, 58, 59; difficulties with Isabella's family, 60–64, 71; prepares home at Pinner, 65–70, 71–78; marriage and honeymoon of, 78–80; visits France, 84–85, 114–115; visits Killarney, 85–87; moves to Greenhithe, 113; visits Germany, 113; moves to new offices in the Strand, 117; extensive activities of, 117–127; inaugurates *The Queen*, 121–123; founds *The Young Englishwoman*, 123; fame as publisher of magazines for boys, 123–125; his grief at Isabella's death, 129–131; sells *The Queen*, 132; failing health of, 133, 173, 174; effect of bank failure on, 133–134; employed by Ward, Lock, and Tyler, 134; forms joint household with the Brownes, 136; dispute with Ward, Lock, and Tyler, 139–143; his part in the Republican craze, 144, 146–157; letters to his sons, 159–163, 173–174; visits Italy, 163–164; starts afresh as publisher, 164; association with T. P. O'Connor, 168–172; T. P.'s description of, 169; final illness and death of, 174–175.

Beeton, Samuel Orchart, jun., 82–83, 115

Beeton, Samuel Powell (father of S. O. Beeton), 16, 18, 29, 58
Beeton, Mrs Samuel Powell, I (mother of S. O. Beeton), 18, 29
Beeton, Mrs Samuel Powell, II (Eliza Dowse), 18, 29, 58, 70, 71, 80, 112
Beeton, Victoria (stepsister of S. O. Beeton), 63
Beeton's Book of Universal Etiquette, 164–167
Beeton's Boy's Own Journal, 73, 74
Beeton's Christmas Annuals, 117, 126, 139–143, 146–157, 165
Beeton's Dictionary of Universal Information, 102, 125
Beeton's Illuminated Family Bible, 125–126, 133
Benedict, Sir Julius, 59, 85
Benjamin Disraeli, Earl of Beaconsfield (O'Connor), 171–172
Bennett, C. H., 126
Bentinck, Lord George, 24–25, 26
Bentley, Richard, 38–39
Berlin, 113
Biarritz, 80
Blair Atholl (racehorse), 114
Blanchard, W., 126
Bogue, David, 32, 36
Bohn, Henry George, 32, 39
Book of Household Management, 59, 83, 87, 88–111, 133, 153, 157; on the domestic virtues, 91; its account of a day's routine, 91–97; on morning calls, 92–93; on dinner-table etiquette, 94–96; on introductions at parties, 96–97; on evenings at home, 97–99; on position of mistress of house, 99–100; on kitchen duties, 100–101; origins of recipes, 102–105; its remarks on pigs, 106–107; success of, 109–111
Bookselling and publishing in the 1850's, 31–33
Bordeaux, 80
Bosworth, Thomas, 41, 43, 57
Boucicault, Dion, 85
Boyhood of Great Men, The (Edgar), 51–52
Boy's Monthly Magazine, The, 117, 124
Boy's Own Magazine, The, 50–54, 57, 117, 124

Boy's Penny Magazine, The, 117, 124
Bradlaugh, Charles, 145, 146
Brentwood (Essex), 29
Brough, J. C., 126
Brougham, Henry, Lord Brougham and Vaux, 31
Browne, Charles R., 136, 158, 177
Browne, Mrs Matilda ("Mamma"), 136–137, 158, 160, 167–168, 173–174, 177
Burnand, Sir Francis C., 126

CAMBRIDGE, GEORGE, DUKE OF, 155
Captain Kyd, The Wizard of the Sea (Ingraham), 173
Captain Master's Children (Hood), 52
Carlyle, Thomas, 30
Carr, Rev. C. R., 158, 160, 177
Cassell and Co., Ltd, 39, 170
Chamberlain, Joseph, 145
Chamberlain, Joseph, senior, 17
Chapman and Hall, 31
Cheapside, 15, 16–17. *See also* Milk Street
Clarke, Charles H., 30, 36, 37, 38, 39, 57
Clarke, Charles H., and Co. (later Clarke, Beeton, and Co.), 30, 32, 33, 36–42, 43, 45, 54–57, 117
Claxton, Florence, 120
Cobden, Richard, 83
Colleen Bawn, The (Boucicault), 85
Coming K——, The, 139–140, 147, 148, 153–156
Connaught, Arthur William, Duke of, 155
Cork, 86
Cox, Horace, 132
Cox and Wyman, 116, 132
Cruikshank, George, junior, 126
Crystal Palace, 67, 68

DALSTON (Cumberland), 19
David, Jules, 120
David Garrick (Robertson), 123
De Tessier, Baroness, 81
Derby Day (Frith), 27
Dickens, Charles, 26, 30, 32
Dilke, Sir Charles, 145, 146
Disraeli, Benjamin, Earl of Beaconsfield, 26, 121, 154, 157, 170–171

Dolphin Tavern, Cheapside, 15, 16–18, 19, 29, 58, 112, 129 n.
Doré, Gustave, 124
Dorling, Frank, 60, 61
Dorling, Henry, 21–22, 24–28, 58, 62, 79, 137
Dorling, Henry Mayson, 21 n., 130
Dorling, Jessie, 79
Dorling, Lucy (Mrs W. H. Smiles), 60, 61, 79 and n., 81, 104, 132, 178
Dorling, Walter, 60, 61
Dorling, William, 22–23, 79
Dowse, Eliza—see Beeton, Mrs Samuel Powell II
Dowty, A. A., 139, 140, 141, 148, 153, 163, 164, 175–176, 178
Doyle, Sir Arthur Conan, 109
Dresden, 114
Dublin, 86
Duet with an Occasional Chorus, A (Doyle), 109

EDGAR, J. G., 51–52, 122
Edinburgh, Alfred, Duke of, 151, 155
Edinburgh, Marie, Duchess of, 151
Edward VII, King, 146–147, 148, 150, 153, 155–157
Edward VII, 153–156
Emerson, S. R., 139, 140
English, Mrs, 81–82
Englishwoman's Cookery Book, The, 89
Englishwoman's Domestic Magazine, The, 44 n., 52, 53, 57, 117, 123, 168; founding of, 45–49; introduction of paper dress patterns in, 46, 85, 120; "Cupid's Letter Bag" in, 48–49, 87; The Scarlet Letter serialized in, 49; Mrs Beeton's cookery notes in, 81; coloured fashion plates in, 83, 85, 87, 120–121; enlarged series of, 119–121; Mrs Matilda Browne editress of, 136, 158
Epsom, 22–28, 58, 59, 60–63, 78–79, 137
Epsom Grand Stand Association, 23–25
"European Library" (Bogue), 32
Exmouth, 158, 173, 177

Famous Regiments (Adams), 51
Famous Ships of the British Navy (Adams), 51

Fijiad, The, 140
Foster, Birket, 46
Fowler, Mr (Beeton's Paris agent), 84
Frith, William, P. 27

Gambler's Wife, The (Pickering), 55
Gard, Mr (friend of Beeton), 159 and n., 162, 163
Gladstone, W. E., 119, 149
Goubaud, Adolph, 84, 85, 120, 130, 161 n., 168
Great Finborough (Suffolk), 15–16
Great Metropolitan Handicap, 16–17, 18, 118
Great Orton (Cumberland), 19, 20
Greenhithe, 113, 127, 136, 158–162, 173
Greenwood, Frederick, 37–38, 39–40, 41 n., 52, 121–122
Greenwood, James, 51, 52, 121, 124
Guards, The (Rafter), 54

HADLEIGH (Essex), 29
Hamilton, Lord Frederick, 55
Hawthorne, Nathaniel, 49
Heidelberg, 59, 80
Henley, L. C., 124
Herbert, Auberon, 145
Hildreth, R., 55
Holmes, Oliver Wendell, 44
Hood, Tom, the younger, 51, 52, 124, 126
Household Words, 26–27
Houssaye, Arsène, 54
Hunt, Thomasin (Mrs John Beeton), 15

INGRAHAM, JOSEPH HOLT, 173

JERRAM, ELIZABETH—see Mayson, Mrs Benjamin
Jerram, William, 19
Jerram, Mrs William ("Granny Jerram"), 19, 21, 28
Jerrold, Evelyn, 140, 141, 148, 153–154, 168, 176
Jewett, John P., 35, 42 and n.
Jockey Club, 24
Jon Duan, 140–141, 146–147, 150–153, 167

Key to Uncle Tom's Cabin, The (Stowe), 43, 56–57
Killarney, 85–87
Knollys, Francis, first Viscount, 155

LAWSON, LUCY (Mrs Samuel Beeton), 16, 18
Lecky, W. E. H., 86
Leech, Henry, 46
Leopold, Prince (later Duke of Albany), 155
Life of Nelson (Southey), 54
Lily of Killarney, The (Boucicault-Benedict), 85
Lind, Jenny, 60, 104
London's Great Outing : The Derby Carnival, 137
Longchamps racecourse, 114–115
Longfellow, Henry Wadsworth, 44, 55
Longman, Thomas, 88
Longmans, Green, and Co., Ltd, 31, 88
Lorne, John Douglas Sutherland, Marquess of, 155
Low, Sampson, and Son, 43, 57
Lowell, James Russell, 44

MACAULAY, LORD, 31, 44
Maccabeus (racehorse), 24
Mackenzie, Sir Morell, 174–175
Macmillan and Co., Ltd, 31
Maddick, George, 118
Malins, Sir Richard, 141–143, 164–167
Manuscript found in a Bottle (Poe), 49
Marengo, 102
Martineau, Harriet, 109
Marvel, Ik, 54
Mayson, Benjamin (father of Mrs Beeton), 19, 20, 21 *n.*, 58
Mayson, Mrs Benjamin (later Dorling), 19–22, 27–28, 58, 67, 71
Mayson, Esther, 21 *and n.*
Mayson, Rev. John (grandfather of Mrs Beeton), 19, 20–21
Mayson, Mrs John, 19 *and n.*
Memorable Battles in English History (Adams), 51
Milk Street, Cheapside, 15, 16–17, 21, 29, 58, 72, 76
Modern Cookery (Acton), 88

Moniteur de la Mode, Le, 120
Mount Pleasant, Greenhithe, 113, 127, 136, 158
Mrs Beeton's Book of Household Management—see *Book of Household Management*
Mrs Beeton's Dictionary of Everyday Cookery, 127–128, 130
Mudie's Library, 30
Murray, John, 31
Myra's Journal of Dress and Fashion, 167–168

NAPLES, 163–164
Napoleon I, 102–103
Napoleon III, 136
"Nasby, Petroleum V.," 125
Newmarket, 81, 82, 115

O'CONNOR, T. P., 155, 168–172
Orchart, Helen (Mrs Samuel Powell Beeton I), 18, 29
Orchart, Thomas, 18
Orleans, 80
Orpwood, Mr (cook), 82
Overend, Gurney, and Co., 133–134

PAGET, LORD HENRY, 155
Pall Mall Gazette, 37, 52, 121
Paper Duty, repeal of, 119
Paris, 80, 84–85, 132, 136
Paxton, Sir Joseph, 67
Philosophers and Actresses, etc. (Houssaye), 54
"Phiz," 137
Pinner, 65–66, 67, 69, 72, 75, 80, 104, 112–113
Poe, Edgar Allan, 49, 54
Poulet à la Marengo, origin of, 102–103
Publishing and bookselling in the 1850's, 31–33
Putnam's (G. P.) Sons, 35
Pyrenees, 80

Queen, The, 117, 121–123, 132

RAFTER, CAPTAIN, 54
Rands, W. B., 51, 122, 124, 126
"Readable Books" series, 36, 40, 54
Reform Bill (1832), 31

Reid, Captain Mayne, 51, 124
Reveries of a Bachelor (Marvel), 54
Rifle Rangers, The (Reid), 51
Robertson, T. W., 123
Robinson, Mrs Maria, 122
Routledge, George, 32
Routledge and Sons (later Routledge and Kegan Paul, Ltd), 39
Running Rein (racehorse), 24
Russell, Sir William Howard, 155

Scalp Hunters, The (Reid), 51
Scarlet Letter, The (Hawthorne), 49
Scott, Clement, 124
Scott, Sir Walter, 95
Self-Help (Smiles), 31
Senn, Hermann, 103
Sherwood, Robert, 59
Siliad, The, 140, 149
Slavery Poems (Longfellow, Southey, Whittier), 55
Smiles, Samuel, 31, 79 *n.*
Smiles, Sir Walter, 79 *n.*
Smiles, W. H., 79 *n.*
Smiles, Mrs W. H.—*see* Dorling, Lucy
Smith, Elder, and Co., 31
Smith, James, 16
Smith, W. H., and Son, 32, 152
Soup à la cantatrice, 104
Soup à la Solferino, origin of, 103
Southey, Robert, 54, 55
Sporting Life, The, 114, 117–118
Sportsman, The, 16
Stagg, William, 129 *and n.*
Standard, The, 120, 127
Stowe, Harriet Beecher, 33–35, 38, 41–44, 55–56
Surplice (racehorse), 26
Swinburne, Algernon C., 42, 155

Tales of Mystery, Imagination, and Humour (Poe), 54
Tennant, Sir Charles, 19 *n.*
Tennant, Margaret (Mrs Robert Trimble), 19 *n.*

Tennyson, Alfred, Lord, 31, 139, 148
Thackeray, W. M., 30, 32
Thomas, W. L., 123
Thomson, Gordon, 124
Thursby (Cumberland), 19, 21
Tillotson, John, 132
Trimble, Isabella (Mrs John Mayson), 19 *and n.*
Trimble, Robert, 19 *n.*
Tyler, Charles, 140, 159 *and n.*, 173

Uncle Tom's Cabin (Stowe), 33–45, 49, 55, 56–57, 122, 132, 153

VICTORIA, QUEEN, 144–147, 150–151, 153, 154–155, 157
Vizetelly, Henry, 36–38, 40–41, 54, 55, 57
Vulliamy, Benjamin, 103 *and n.*

"WARD, ARTEMUS," 44, 125, 132
Ward, Lock, and Tyler (later Ward, Lock, and Co., Ltd), 134–136, 139–143, 150, 164–167
Warne, Frederick, 32, 39, 40
Weaklin, Frederick, 80, 138
Weekly Despatch, The, 137–138
Weir, Harrison, 46, 124
Weldon, C. E., 135–136, 137–138, 140, 164, 168
Wetherell, Elizabeth, 55
What Does She Do With It? (pamphlet), 146
White Slave, The (Hildreth), 55
Whittier, J. G., 55
Wide, Wide World, The (Wetherell), 55
Wild Dayrell (racehorse), 59
Wood, Rev. J. G., 132
Wyatt, Isaac, 18, 112
Wyatt, Mrs Isaac—*see* Beeton, Mrs Samuel Powell II

YOUNG, FRANCIS, 115, 132
Young Englishwoman, The, 115–116, 117, 123, 136, 158, 167, 168
Youth's Instructor, 53

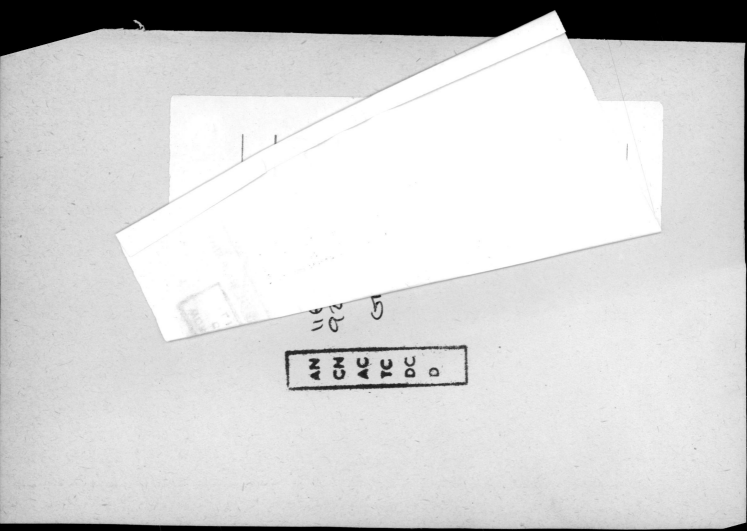